# RENEWABLE ENERGY

## POWER THE WORLD WITH SUSTAINABLE FUEL

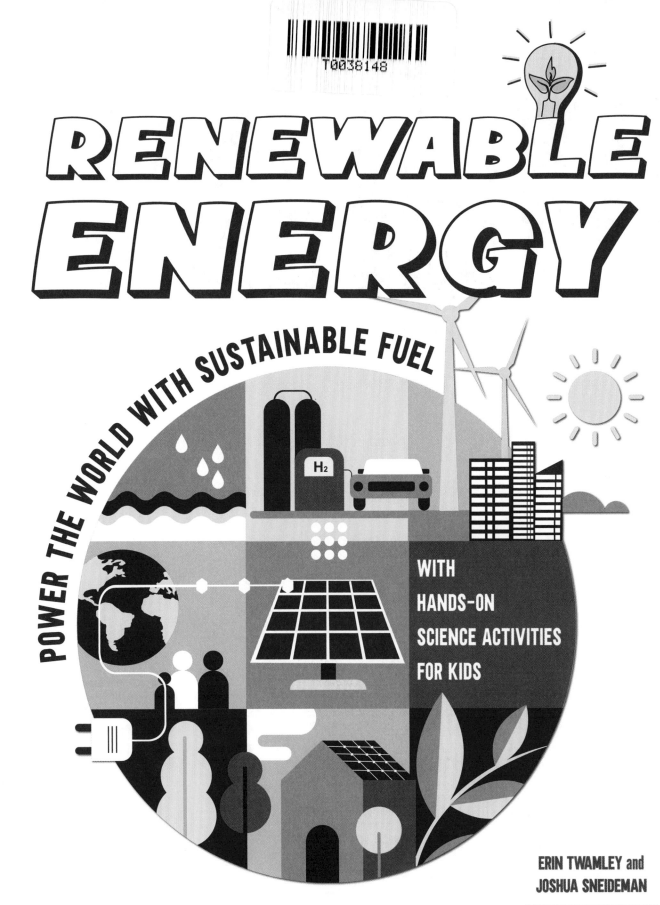

H₂

WITH
HANDS-ON
SCIENCE ACTIVITIES
FOR KIDS

**ERIN TWAMLEY** and
**JOSHUA SNEIDEMAN**

ILLUSTRATED BY MICAH RAUCH

## More science titles from Nomad Press

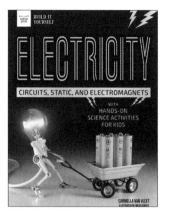

Check out more titles at www.nomadpress.net

Nomad Press

A division of Nomad Communications

10 9 8 7 6 5 4 3 2 1

This book was manufactured by Versa Press, East Peoria, Illinois
April 2024, Job #J23-59083
ISBN Softcover: 978-1-64741-119-0
ISBN Hardcover: 978-1-64741-116-9

Educational Consultant, Marla Conn

Questions regarding the ordering of this book should be addressed to
Nomad Press
PO Box 1036, Norwich, VT 05055
www.nomadpress.net

Printed in the United States.

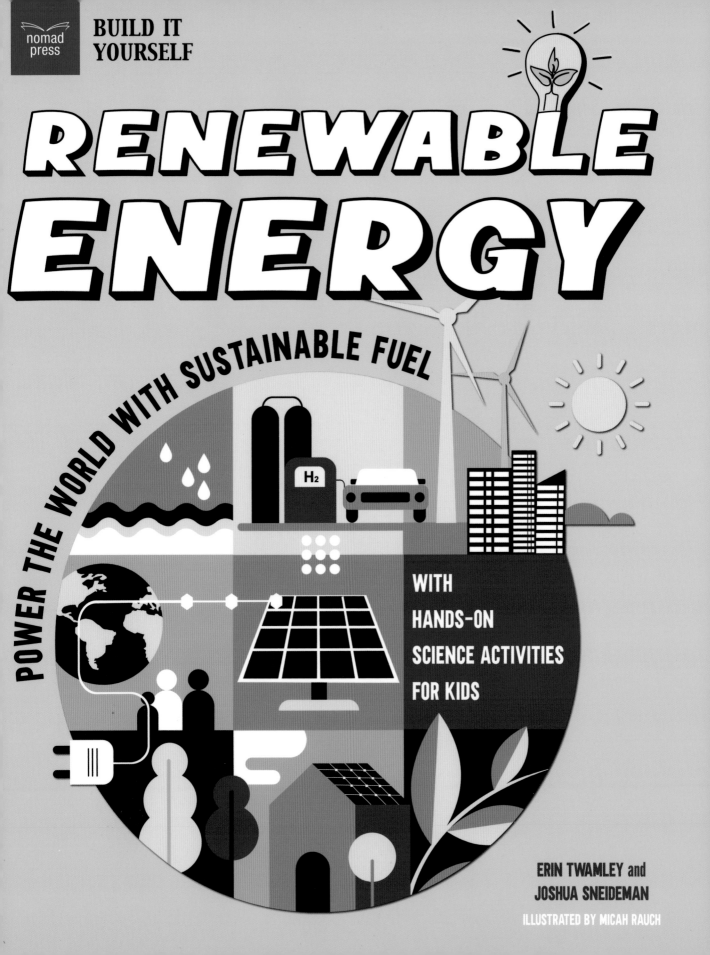

nomad press

BUILD IT YOURSELF

# RENEWABLE ENERGY

## POWER THE WORLD WITH SUSTAINABLE FUEL

H₂

WITH
HANDS-ON
SCIENCE ACTIVITIES
FOR KIDS

ERIN TWAMLEY and
JOSHUA SNEIDEMAN

ILLUSTRATED BY MICAH RAUCH

# CONTENTS

**Interested in Primary Sources? Look for this icon.**

Some of the QR codes in this book link to primary sources that offer firsthand information about the topic. Many photos are considered primary sources because a photograph takes a picture at the moment something happens. Use a smartphone or tablet app to scan the QR code and explore more! You can find a list of the URLs on the Resources page. You can also use the suggested keywords to find other helpful sources.

🔎 renewable energy

**200 BCE:** One of the first windmills is invented in Persia, in present-day Iran.

**600 BCE:** Greek thinker Thales discovers static electricity after rubbing amber and silk together. He notes the electric charge created and the attraction of objects.

**2000 BCE:** The Chinese are the first to use coal as an energy source.

**1600 CE:** William Gilbert of England coins the term *electricity* from *elektron*, the Greek word for "amber."

**1748:** Commercial coal production begins in the United States in Richmond, Virginia.

**1752:** Benjamin Franklin discovers electricity.

**1767:** French-Swiss scientist Horace de Saussure makes the first recorded attempt to use a solar cooker to cook food.

**1800:** At this point in U.S. history, American homes consume most of the country's energy.

**1805:** The world population reaches 1 billion people.

**1821:** The first natural gas well in the United States is drilled.

**1881:** The coal-fired, steam-powered railway train becomes the worldwide standard for passenger travel.

**1882:** Thomas Edison builds the first hydroelectric dam in New York, near Niagara Falls.

**1892:** Boise, Idaho, is powered by America's first geothermal energy heating system.

**1893:** The first biofuel car engine debuts.

**1935:** The Hoover Dam, the world's largest hydroelectric power plant, is built in Arizona.

**1948:** The Dover Sun House in Massachusetts is the first occupied solar-powered house in the United States.

**1959:** The world population reaches 3 billion people.

**1977:** The U.S. Department of Energy is created as a new federal government agency.

**1979:** Solar panels are installed on the roof of the White House.

**1980:** The world's first wind farm opens in New Hampshire.

**1982:** Australian Hans Tholstrup drives the first solar-powered car—the *Quiet Achiever*—almost 2,800 miles.

**2005:** The concept of the personal carbon footprint is introduced by British Petroleum.

**2007:** The U.S. Green Jobs Act is implemented.

**2011:** The total energy use per person in the United States is about 313 million British thermal units (Btu). The total energy use per person across the globe is 75 million Btu.

**2013:** The first hydrogen fuel cell automobile is for sale from Hyundai.

**2015:** The U.S. Clean Power Plan comes into effect, imposing the first nationwide limits on carbon dioxide emissions from power plants.

**2016:** The first offshore wind farm begins operating off Rhode Island's Block Island.

**2022:** Solar energy systems are located at more than 7,300 K-12 schools across the United States.

**2023:** The world population reaches 8 billion.

**2050:** All the world's power could be generated by renewable energy.

# POWERING
# OUR PLANET

Look around your house. Are the lights on? Is someone watching television? Is a cell phone charging? We use **energy** every day to power our world. Most of the energy we need comes from burning **fossil fuels**, which are **nonrenewable energy** sources. For our future, however, we are looking toward **renewable energy** sources that naturally replenish themselves.

## ESSENTIAL QUESTION

Why is it important to find and use renewable energy sources in place of fossil fuels?

## WORDS TO KNOW

**energy:** the ability or power to do work or cause change.

**fossil fuels:** coal, oil, and natural gas. These energy sources come from the fossils of plants and animals that lived millions of years ago.

**nonrenewable energy:** a form of energy that can be used up, that we can't make more of, such as oil.

**renewable energy:** a form of energy that naturally replenishes itself, including the energy of the sun or the wind.

1

# RENEWABLE ENERGY

**pollution:** harmful materials that damage the air, water, and soil.

**climate change:** a change in the long-term average weather patterns of a place.

**sustainable:** a process or resource that can be used without being completely used up or destroyed.

**technology:** the tools, methods, and systems used to solve a problem or do work.

**solar energy:** energy from the sun.

**wind energy:** energy from the wind that can be transformed into electricity.

**hydropower:** energy produced by the movement of water.

**geothermal energy:** energy from below Earth's surface that can heat or cool using differences in temperature above and below ground.

**bioenergy:** energy created from recently living matter, such as trees and other plants.

**engineering:** the use of science and math in the design and construction of things.

**turbine:** a machine with rotating blades that changes one type of energy to another, such as wind energy into electricity.

**electricity:** a form of energy caused by the movement of tiny particles that powers lights, appliances, and many other electric devices.

Renewable energy is competing against fossil fuels, which have dominated the energy industry for the past 150 years. We need energy to power everything from heat and air conditioning to cars, cellphones, and video games. The burning of fossil fuels causes **pollution** and **climate change** and is not **sustainable**. Using renewable energies will help restore a cleaner and greener planet.

Every day, new scientific discoveries are made and new **technology** created from what we learn. These technologies allow us to develop and improve renewable energy sources that produce clean energy and end our reliance on fossil fuels.

In this book, we'll investigate five different renewable energies—**solar**, **wind**, **hydropower**, **geothermal**, and **bioenergy**. We'll also learn about the passion and hard work of people who work in the fields of science, technology, and **engineering**.

These renewable energy technologies are moving **us toward a single shared goal—a cleaner future.**

## A RENEWABLE HISTORY

Humans have been looking to the world around them for energy solutions for a long time—thousands of years!

Wind was used as a power source more than 7,000 years ago. Ancient Egyptians harnessed the wind to propel boats along the Nile River in Egypt.

Around 3,000 years ago, the Persians began using wind power to pump water and grind grain. Now, we see wind **turbines** dotting the horizon all over the world to produce the **electricity** we rely on.

## The Scientific Method

A scientific method worksheet is a useful tool for keeping your ideas and observations organized. The scientific method is the process scientists use to ask and answer questions. Use a notebook as a science journal to make a scientific method worksheet for each experiment you do.

**Question:** What are we trying to find out? What problem are we trying to solve?

**Research:** What is already known about this topic?

**Hypothesis:** What do we think the answer will be?

**Equipment:** What supplies are we using?

**Method:** What procedure are we following?

**Results:** What happened and why?

# RENEWABLE ENERGY

Water is another energy source that humans have been using to perform work for thousands of years. The Greeks used **water wheels** for grinding wheat into flour more than 2,000 years ago.

A little closer to our time—1880—a water turbine first powered 16 electric lights in a theater in Grand Rapids, Michigan. Today, hydropower is the most widely used renewable energy source around the world, available in more than 150 countries.

Solar power is not new, either. Its history spans nearly 3,000 years, from the seventh century **BCE** to today. At first, humans used glass and mirrors to concentrate the sun's heat to light fires. Now, we use **solar panels** to convert the sun's energy into electricity.

## Nuclear Energy

There are two types of **nuclear energy—nuclear fission** and **nuclear fusion**. We have been harnessing electricity from nuclear fission for decades. At nuclear power plants, heat to **generate** electricity is created when **atoms** are split apart. This is called fission. In most cases, the fuel used for nuclear fission is uranium. Uranium is a nonrenewable **resource** and nuclear fission produces radioactive waste that is highly dangerous.

Scientists from more than 50 countries have been trying to force atoms together in a process called nuclear fusion. Nuclear fusion is what powers the stars and gives the sun its energy. The hope is that this method will result in a clean and safe renewable resource.

The ISS uses solar energy to power the astronauts' lives in space!
Credit: NASA

The first known use of geothermal energy occurred more than 10,000 years ago in North America. People used water from hot springs for cooking, bathing, and cleaning. Now, we use geothermal energy to heat and cool buildings with **geothermal heat pumps** and can even generate electricity in geothermal power plants.

**Solar panels can be found in many places, from light poles here on Earth to the International Space Station (ISS).**

Bioenergy is produced from **biomass** such as wood. In fact, wood is the oldest form of bioenergy and was the main source of energy in the world until the mid-1800s. Today, billions of people still use wood for cooking and heating. In 2021, the United States exported about 8 million tons of wood fuel pellets. The use of biomass fuels for transportation and electricity generation is increasing in many developed countries. We use biofuels such as ethanol and biodiesel. We can even take food grease, animal waste, and garbage and convert them into usable forms of energy called biogas, or methane. Because bioenergy can come in different forms, including solid, liquid, and gas, we are seeing its diverse use throughout the world.

**Industrial Revolution:** a period during the eighteenth and nineteenth centuries when large cities and factories began to replace small towns and farming.

**environment:** everything in nature, living and nonliving, including plants, animals, soil, rocks, and water.

**fossil:** the remains of any living thing, including animals and plants, that have been preserved in rock.

**carbon:** a kind of atom that is the building block of most living things, as well as diamonds, charcoal, and graphite.

**emission:** something that is sent or given out, such as smoke, gas, heat, or light.

**atmosphere:** the mixture of gases surrounding Earth.

**greenhouse gases:** gases in the earth's atmosphere that trap heat.

**acid rain:** rain that contains pollution from burning fuels.

**smog:** fog combined with smoke or other pollutants.

**toxic:** poisonous, harmful, or deadly.

From the mid-1700s to the mid-1800s, the **Industrial Revolution** saw the discovery and invention of new science and technology, such as our ability to burn fossil fuels. At that point, our modern way of life and its rapid expansion became powered mostly by fossil fuels. Coal was used for steam-powered boats to travel the Mississippi River, for trains to travel coast to coast, and in factories to make steel. People didn't realize that fossil fuels came with a high price—climate change and other problems.

Now, the use of renewable energies is expanding thanks to advances in the science and technology used to harness this energy. People want to protect their health and the **environment** by reducing the burning of fossil fuels. The urgent need to fight climate change is pushing us to make breakthroughs in the field of renewable energy.

About 64 percent of the **world's electricity comes** from burning fossil fuels.

## FOSSIL FUELS

To better understand the importance of renewable energy, we need to know more about the fossil fuels we are trying to leave behind. Coal, oil, and natural gas are called fossil fuels because they come from animal and plant **fossils**. The energy held in those ancient plants and animals came from the sun millions of years ago. Our planet of 8 billion people runs mostly on energy from fossil fuels. People burn fossil fuels to create the energy we need to drive cars, power computers, heat and cool homes, and refrigerate food.

Fossil fuels are found everywhere on the planet, from the oceans to deserts, from the Arctic to the tropics. When we use this energy to cook our food, drive our cars, and make electricity, we are using a kind of solar energy and releasing stored **carbon** from millions of years ago.

Humans have been using fossil fuels since the 1700s. But burning fossil fuels **harms the planet and human health by causing** pollution that damages our air, water, and climate.

When coal-fired power plants generate electricity, they release harmful **emissions** into the **atmosphere**. These include **greenhouse gases** such as carbon dioxide and methane, plus other harmful gases that cause **acid rain**, **smog**, and health problems. **Toxic** metals such as mercury, lead, arsenic, and cadmium are also released and are known to cause birth defects and other health problems.

Power plants that use solar, wind, water, nuclear, or geothermal energy to generate electricity do not release the harmful chemicals that burning fossil fuels creates.

## WORDS TO KNOW

**energy transition:** a period during which the dominant resource used to produce energy is replaced by other resources.

**global warming:** a gradual increase in the average temperature of Earth's atmosphere and its oceans.

**carbon dioxide ($CO_2$):** a gas formed by the burning of fossil fuels, the rotting of plants and animals, and the breathing out of animals, including humans.

**current:** the steady flow of water in one direction or the flow of electricity.

## THE ENERGY TRANSITION

Both the search for fossils fuels and the use of these energy sources hurt our planet. Our global energy use is responsible for about two-thirds of greenhouse gas emissions. The movement away from using fossil fuels to renewable energy is called an **energy transition**. This is a global effort to change how we power our lifestyles.

More than half of the renewable **energy used in the United States** goes to generating electricity.

The future of our planet is uncertain. The threat of climate change is very real. Climate change affects every region, from tiny remote islands to whole countries. About 97 percent of scientists agree that burning fossil fuels is responsible for **global warming** and climate change. Renewable energy power plants can help us generate electricity without releasing harmful substances.

## Climate Change History

Eunice Foote (1819–1888) was the first scientist to make the connection between the amount of **carbon dioxide ($CO_2$)** in our atmosphere and climate change. Her research and experiments measured carbon dioxide levels as early as 1856. Scientists such as Charles David Keeling (1928–2005) used her work to continue to measure carbon dioxide levels. Today, we measure not only carbon dioxide, but also other greenhouse gases in our atmosphere. The level of greenhouse gases has been rapidly rising and is far higher now than during any period in Earth's history. To fight climate change, we must lower our release of greenhouse gases.

The sun will keep providing energy for millions of years. The wind is always going to blow. The ocean has regular tides, waves, and **currents** that could help power our lives. A new generation of scientists and farmers can produce green liquid fuels from plants for our cars. Geothermal power, originating at the center of Earth, will last as long as our planet. This inner heat is being used to warm some of the coldest places on Earth.

**Watch this animated TED-Ed video,** *A Guide to the Energy of the Earth.* How does energy cycle through our planet, from the sun to our food chain to electricity? What are some ways these are all connected?

TED-Ed Guide Energy Earth

The need to move from nonrenewable fossil fuels to renewable energy sources is urgent. Right now, we are in an energy transition trying to change how we generate and use energy. Rapid advances in technology are allowing us to use more clean, green, and sustainable energy sources. We need people like you to help us transition.

Today, more than 30 percent of all electricity worldwide comes from renewable sources. In 2014, only 10 percent of our total energy consumption came from renewable sources. We're heading in the right direction!

*TEXT TO* **WORLD**

What kind of heat source do you have at your school? Does the heat come from renewable energy?

## It's Personal

What's a way that you can support the energy transition right now? Use your knowledge of energy to ask questions about how energy is used in your home or school. For example, what kind of light bulbs are being used? Do you **recycle** or **compost**? Do you use reusable bags while shopping? By asking questions about energy use, we can better understand the ways we can make changes.

Is one renewable energy source better than the rest? That depends on many different factors, and no energy source is 100-percent perfect. Each comes with its own tradeoffs and impacts on the environment. As we learn about the different sources of renewable energy, we'll examine these tradeoffs and how they impact us and our planet.

One thing is clear—together, these renewable energy technologies can help us move away from our dependence on fossil fuels. Renewable energy will improve our planet's health and our own!

Our investigation into renewable energies begins with a look at solar energy. Let's explore the incredible energy from the sun that has powered our planet for the past 4.5 billion years.

## Essential Questions

Each chapter of this book begins with an essential question to help guide your exploration of energy. Keep the question in mind as you read the chapter. At the end of each chapter, use your science journal to record your thoughts and answers.

### ESSENTIAL QUESTION

Why is it important to find and use renewable energy sources in place of fossil fuels?

# ENERGY
# INVESTIGATOR

Energy is the ability to do work or make change. Energy is invisible, but we know when it's working! Do you turn off the lights when you leave a room? How many devices do you charge? Everything you do requires energy. Look for energy clues all around your home or classroom. Find objects and mark them with a Post-it note to see all the things around you that use energy.

> **Look all around your home or classroom.** Identify what is using energy. Mark what is using energy with a Post-it note.

> **After 10 minutes, make observations about all the things using energy.** How many ways do you use energy in your home or classroom? Can you spot ways to use less energy?

**Using renewable energy such as wind and solar saves water. Nearly 60,000 gallons of water per megawatt hour (MWh) of electricity are used to produce gas, coal, or nuclear energy.**

## Try This!

Take this online energy literacy quiz to test your knowledge about energy. What can you do to learn more about energy?

🔎 Energy Literacy Quiz

## Measuring Energy

We use different units to measure different types of energy.

> The brightness of light bulbs is measured in **lumens**. The more lumens, the brighter the light.

> Electricity can be measured in **watts**, which is a unit of power measured over time: 1 kilowatt (kW) is 1,000 watts; 1 megawatt (MW) is 1,000,000 watts, enough electricity to power 650 houses; 1 gigawatt (GW) is 1,000,000,000 watts, enough electricity to power 650,000 homes.

> Gasoline, diesel, biofuels, and other liquid fuels are measured in barrels: 1 barrel equals 42 gallons.

> Coal and other solid fuels are measured in tons: 1 ton equals 2,000 pounds.

# EXPLORE
# ENERGY!

**TOOL KIT**
- paper
- scissors
- tape
- drinking straws

We use energy for everything! Explore energy with soda straw rockets you can make yourself.

**Caution:** Have an adult help you with this project. Safety first!

> **Cut out a paper rectangle about the length of a drinking straw.** Wrap the paper around a pencil and tape it in the shape of a tube.

> **Twist and pinch the top of your rocket around the pencil tip.** Tape it in a cone shape so no air can escape through it.

> **Slide your pencil out—you should now have a thin hollow tube with a pointed tip.** That's your rocket!

> **Insert a drinking straw through the open end.** Aim your rocket and blow! What happens? How far does your rocket fly?

## Try This!

Cut out triangles and tape them to your rocket as tail fins. Does this change how your rocket flies? Try making your rocket out of heavier paper. Do you need to blow harder to get it to fly? What does this tell you about how much energy is needed to move things of different sizes?

## Climate Change Hero

Eden Full is a young solar innovator best known for her invention of the SunSaluter. The SunSaluter is a non-toxic, inexpensive, recyclable device made of metal and bamboo that allows solar panels to track the sun without using a motor. The SunSaluter includes solar panels that rotate to track the sun using mechanical water flow, giving users 40 percent more electricity. Today, her invention provides clean water using solar energy for rural communities without access to electricity in 18 countries.

 Listen to her TED talk about how she developed her invention and her intentions for its use. How do her experiences in the world affect what and how she invents?

🔍 Eden Full TEDxBerkeley

# Chapter 1

# SUNLIGHT, SUNLIGHT,
# IS IT TOO BRIGHT?

People have been using solar power since the beginning of human history, but it's only recently that we've developed technologies to capture the energy of the sun. Scientists and engineers are now working to make these technologies more **efficient** and more useful every day.

What is the sun? Most people think of the sun as a featureless, unchanging ball of heat and light, but the sun is a star at the center of our **solar system** that is 4.6 billion years old.

Without the sun, we wouldn't exist!

**ESSENTIAL QUESTION**

How can we use the sun to produce energy here on Earth?

**WORDS TO KNOW**

**efficient:** wasting as little energy as possible.

**solar system:** the sun, the eight planets, and their moons, together with smaller bodies. The planets orbit the sun.

## WORDS TO KNOW

**solar eclipse:** when the moon moves between the sun and the earth, blocking the sun's light.

**satellite:** an object that circles another object in space. Also, a device that circles Earth and transmits information.

**data:** facts and observations about something.

**ultraviolet (UV) light:** a type of light with a short wavelength that can't be seen with the naked eye.

**visible light:** light that the human eye can see.

**infrared light:** an invisible type of light with a longer wavelength than visible light, which can also be felt as heat.

**absorb:** to soak up a liquid or take in energy, heat, light, or sound.

**reflect:** to bounce off and redirect something that hits a surface, such as heat, light, or sound.

**species:** a group of living things that are closely related and can produce young.

**photosynthesis:** the process plants use to convert the sun's energy into food.

**wavelength:** the spacing of sound or light waves.

For centuries, people have studied the sun, tracking its path across the sky and recording events such as **solar eclipses**. In more recent times, scientists at the National Aeronautics and Space Administration (NASA) have studied the sun with **satellites** that collect lots of **data**. This data show that the sun's energy is released in a regular pattern.

Solar energy comes to Earth in the form of rays. The sun emits different kinds of rays, including **ultraviolet (UV) light**, **visible light**, and **infrared light**. Earth's atmosphere **absorbs** some of these rays and **reflects** other rays into space. The rays that are absorbed help warm our atmosphere and make it possible for different **species** of plants and animals to live on Earth.

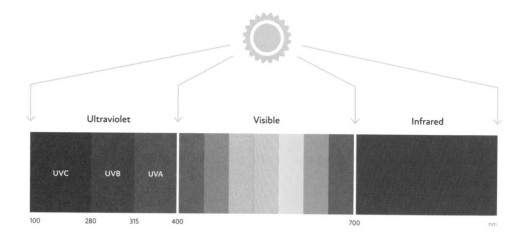

## The Spectrum of Light

Plants absorb light and use it to produce energy through **photosynthesis**. Animals use plant energy for their own energy. Without the sun and plants, animal life would not exist! To use solar energy for our energy needs, we need to figure out how to capture the sun's rays and make them useful. Let's learn more about this process.

## CAPTURING THE SUN

Humans have harnessed solar energy throughout history. We know the sun's rays were used to help build fires as early as 700 BCE. Scholars believe Archimedes (c. 287–c. 212), a Greek mathematician and scientist, developed a "heat ray" weapon around 214–212 BCE that used mirrors to concentrate the sun's energy to burn sails on enemy ships.

### Look Up!

Why is the sky blue? When we look up on a sunny day, we see blue sky because light from the sun travels through oxygen and nitrogen molecules in the atmosphere to get to Earth. Light energy also travels in waves of different colors and lengths. These waves are scattered when they pass through the molecules. Blue waves are scattered more than other colors because their **wavelengths** are shorter. That's why we see blue!

Archimedes is thought to have used heat rays to burn attacking ships during the Siege of Syracuse.

Credit: Giulio Parigi

**photon:** a particle of energy in sunlight.

**photovoltaics:** technology used to convert sunlight into electricity.

**solar thermal:** technology used to heat water with energy from the sun and convert it into electricity.

**matter:** anything that has weight and takes up space. Almost everything is made of matter!

**solar cell:** a device that converts the energy of the sun into electrical energy.

**electron:** a particle in an atom with a negative charge.

**inverter:** a device that converts an electrical charge into a type of electricity that can be used in homes.

**silicon:** an element used in solar panels that can interact with photons to release electrons.

Today, solar energy must be converted into electricity so that we can use it to power our devices and heat our homes. How?

We use solar panels to convert solar energy into the kind of electricity that we access through a wall outlet. The science of solar panels is based on the work of Albert Einstein (1879–1955), who discovered that light is made of **photons**. His 1905 work on light and electricity was important for the development of solar panels. Without his discovery, we would not be able to use solar power.

Now, we can capture the energy using **photovoltaics** and **solar thermal** technology. Let's see how these two technologies work.

The U.S. Department of Energy in Washington, DC, **has solar panels on its rooftop. More than 900 solar panels cover nearly** 2,000 square feet on the roof to help power the building.

**Photovoltaic Effect**

SUNLIGHT

Photon Track

Solar Panels

Anti-reflective Coating

Conductors

Electron Flow

"Hole" Flow

N-Layer Negative Conductor

Crystalline Semiconductor Usually Silicon

P-Layer Positive Conductor

Current

Reflective Coating

Solar water boilers in India

Sunlight is composed of photons, which are tiny particles of solar energy. These photons contain a very specific amount of energy. When traveling through empty space, photons move at the speed of light, about 186,411 miles per second. One of the most important qualities of photons is that they can collide with other **matter**. When photons strike a **solar cell**, they can be absorbed, reflected, or pass through it. When photons are absorbed, **electrons** inside the cell start to move, which creates an electrical current.

**Learn more about the history of solar energy in this video!** What are some innovative ways we might see solar panels used in the future?

🔍 NREL Energy Basics: Solar

That electricity travels to an **inverter**, which changes the current to a type that can be used in your home.

The biggest challenge in using solar energy is creating a solar panel that can transfer photons into electricity efficiently. Scientists, researchers, and engineers are continually working to improve the design and efficiency of solar panels.

**The first solar cells were created in 1954 at Bell Laboratories in New Jersey. Three scientists made these cells from silicon, a common substance found in sand. Silicon is also used to make computer chips.**

## WORDS TO KNOW

**battery:** a device that stores and produces electricity using chemicals.

**solar tracker:** a device that allows mounted solar panels to follow the movement of the sun.

**More than 7,300 schools around the United States are using solar technology!**

The early solar panels from the 1950s were not very efficient. Back then, only 5 percent of the energy that reached a panel's surface was converted into electricity—95 percent of the energy was lost! Through research and innovation, engineers have greatly improved the efficiency of solar panel designs. A solar panel created in 2015 at the National Renewable Energy Laboratory in Colorado keeps up to 45 percent of the sun's energy.

The increased efficiency of solar panels means fewer panels are needed to power a house, business, or city. Consider the Solar Photovoltaic Power Plant in Tangtse, India. High in the Himalayas at nearly 14,500 feet, this plant powers a remote village of about 400 homes. That's a lot of homes using renewable energy! How efficient do you think solar panels will be 50 years from now?

Solar energy produces no pollution and leaves no carbon footprint beyond the production of the solar panels and batteries that are used to store the energy. This makes solar one of the renewables with the most potential for continued growth.

## SOLAR-POWERED TRANSPORTATION

What kind of car does your family drive? It's probably a car that uses gasoline. Or maybe it's a hybrid that uses gasoline and an electric battery. It might even be an electric car. What about a solar-powered car?

For billions of years, light on Earth has been coming from the sun and stars. Today, artificial lights overpower the darkness, and our cities glow at night, even when seen from outer space. Our city lights are brighter than starlight! They are so bright they result in light pollution, which makes it very hard for us to see stars, planets, satellites, comets, and other objects in the sky. Some people are working to make sure we protect dark skies. **You can learn more at this website. What is the light pollution like where you live?**

 Darksky

Today, solar-powered cars are manufactured with solar panels attached to the top of the vehicle. These cars convert sunlight into electricity using photovoltaic cells and send the energy to a **battery** for later use. On average, solar batteries last between 5 to 25 years.

They are environmentally friendly, reduce transportation costs, and have a long lifespan. The first solar-powered car, for sale in 2022, features 1,000 solar panels and has a range of 450 continuous miles at 60 miles per hour (mph).

Many solar-powered cars are used for racing. The first race was in Switzerland in 1985. It was called the Tour de Sol.

**Solar trackers** also help increase the amount of energy produced. **Solar trackers sense the direction of the sun and rotate or** tilt solar panels for maximum exposure to sunlight.

These cars are very expensive to manufacture. They are large to hold the solar panels and batteries needed to go long distances. Although solar cars have been popular to race, there is not an affordable solar-powered car on the market yet.

Tokai University's solar car *Tokai Challenger*

Credit: Hideki Kimura, Kouhei Sagawa (CC BY 3.0)

## WORDS TO KNOW

**aeronautical engineer:** a person who designs and tests aircraft.

**PhD:** stands for doctor of philosophy. A PhD is the highest degree in an area of study given by a college or university.

**physics:** the science of how matter and energy work together.

**concentrated solar power:** when a large amount of solar energy is concentrated using mirrors.

**passive solar power:** the use of black surfaces or pipes to capture the heat of solar energy.

What about flying? In August 2015, the first solar-powered plane flew around the world without using a single drop of fossil fuel. The *Solar Impulse* traveled 25,000 miles during five days and nights of flying nonstop.

For decades, NASA has been using solar panels to power its missions, from satellites that orbit Earth to the International Space Station used for research. Solar power in space isn't new. NASA first used solar power in 1964 on a satellite called Nimbus 1. Aeronautical engineers began designing solar flight vehicles in the 1970s.

Solar panels on a satellite in space

Today, NASA is planning for human spaceflight to Mars with its Orion program. This mission is highly dependent on solar panels for success. Although solar power isn't used to launch rockets in space, solar power is abundant and efficient to keep all systems on board supplied with power while a spacecraft is in space.

## SOLAR THERMAL ENERGY

Engineers have designed another way to capture energy from the sun. Solar thermal energy turns the power of the sun into heat. There are two different types of solar thermal energy systems: **concentrated solar power** and **passive solar power**.

## Katharine Burr Blodgett

Katharine Burr Blodgett (1898–1979) was the first female scientist to earn a **PhD** in **physics** from Cambridge University. She went on to create anti-reflective coatings for glass, including on solar panels, and found ways to make solar panels more efficient and water repellent. Her work has helped make solar panels a leading renewable energy tool.

# RENEWABLE ENERGY

Concentrated solar power uses mirrors to reflect a large area of sunlight onto a smaller area. The mirrors automatically track the sun throughout the day. The concentrated light heats water and converts it to steam. The steam powers a generator that then produces electricity. Concentrated solar power is mainly found in sunny states.

A solar power plant

A solar power tower is one type of concentrated solar power plant. Such a tower can produce temperatures of more than 900 degrees Fahrenheit (482 degrees Celsius). The largest solar power tower is the Ivanpah Solar Electric Generation System. Located in southern California, it uses three towers to produce enough electricity to power 100,000 homes.

In one day, Earth receives more energy from the sun than the **world uses in one year! The sun will make energy for billions** of years. We will never run out of it.

That's great news, but the Ivanpah Solar Power Facility is classified as a greenhouse gas **emitter** by the State of California. Why? Because it has to burn fossil fuels for several hours each morning so that it can quickly reach its operating temperature. Remember, not one renewable energy working alone can provide all the energy needed for everyone.

Can we use solar power at night? Yes! We can't collect the sun's energy **at night, but we can use stored solar energy** from the day. We do this by using a battery. Figuring out how to store the sun's energy in small batteries that **can be used at a later time is the biggest challenge scientists** and engineers are working on!

Another type of concentrated solar power plant uses curved mirrors that reflect the sun's rays to convert water to steam. The mirrors are shaped like half-pipes and are 94-percent reflective.

The sunlight bounces off the mirrors and is directed to a central tube, which heats to more than 750 degrees Fahrenheit (399 degrees Celsius). The reflected light focused on the central tube is 80 times more intense than ordinary sunlight.

## Solar Innovations

Can you imagine if all our windows, sidewalks, driveways, and paths were made of solar panels? Engineers have designed roads and bike paths in places such as the Netherlands and France as well as on some small roads in the United States. Large solar panels float just off the coasts of the United Kingdom, South Korea, and China, powering thousands of homes. Engineers are working on windows covered in solar panels that can power whole office buildings and schools. Solar is one of the fastest growing renewable energy technologies around the world.

# RENEWABLE ENERGY

The heat in the tube is used to boil water. Steam from the boiling water turns a turbine that generates electricity. The Kramer Solar Power Junction facility in California is the world's largest solar array using this technology. This plant can power up to 500,000 homes!

How do we capture the sun's energy with no mechanical or electronic devices? That's called passive solar power. This approach uses black surfaces or pipes to quickly heat water in a process called passive solar water heating. It is used in many places around the world. People run water through black pipes placed on the roofs of their homes to save energy. Opening curtains to let the sun warm the house on a sunny but cold day is a good, everyday example of passive solar power.

A large solar farm

## POWERING OUR LIVES WITH THE SUN

Solar technologies are used around the world. The first solar-paneled home was built in the United States in 1948 in Massachusetts, and the first solar panels were installed on the U.S. White House under President Jimmy Carter in 1979. More recently, the Vatican installed 2,400 solar panels in 2008. The solar industry has been growing tremendously.

Businesses, homes, energy utilities, and schools are joining the solar revolution. More than 5 million students in the United States attend schools that use forms of solar technology. All around the world, massive solar farms are being built to take advantage of our ever-present sun.

Solar power isn't just an environmental convenience. It can also help save lives. Nearly 1 billion people around the world are still living without electricity.

This includes thousands of families living on tribal lands in the United States. The houses there don't have light switches and power outlets. Many families still burn wood to heat their homes, cook their food, and light their homes at night. Fires can grow out of control and create a burning hazard—plus, the smoke particles emitted by open fires are bad for people's health.

### Solar Jobs

Solar jobs can take place in an office, a research lab, on a solar farm, or even on a rooftop. Researchers ask questions, run experiments, and work to solve some of our greatest energy challenges, such as storing solar energy. Scientists study the connections between the environment and solar energy. Engineers design and build solar systems around the world. Technicians and installers are hands-on experts at repairing and maintaining solar energy projects. Solar jobs require knowledge and skills in science, technology, engineering, art, and math. You might have heard these subjects called STEM or **STEAM** subjects. STEM jobs, especially in renewable energy, are fast growing and diverse.

Look around your neighborhood. Do you see any solar panels? You might see them on the roofs of buildings or free standing in fields or yards. In the countryside, you might even see solar farms that are the size of football fields. Solar panels can power streetlights, parking garages, houses, businesses, calculators, and even radios.

We need engineers and scientists to continue to improve solar technology and leaders who demand change. The more solar energy we have available, the healthier our planet will be.

## SOLAR ENERGY TRADEOFFS

Solar energy offers incredible potential for the future. But no single energy source is perfect. Solar energy has pros but also potential cons. What are some of the tradeoffs of switching to solar energy?

Cities absorb a lot of solar energy because of all the black **surfaces on roads and buildings, so cities are often hotter than the surrounding** countryside. This is why scientists call cities "heat islands." Green spaces within cities are much cooler. Compare summer **temperatures in Central Park with those in the developed parts of New York City.**

## Solar Power in Flight

The airports of the future are here, and they're powered by the sun. From parking garages to terminal operations, solar can help us take flight. Airports across the United States are using solar panels to generate power. The Chattanooga Metropolitan Airport in Tennessee is the first airport in the United States to generate all the power it needs through a solar farm of nearly 10,000 panels.

**Watch this news story about the airport. Why is it important for the solar energy savings to offset the costs? How does that motivate businesses to use solar power?**

🔎 Chattanooga airport solar video

# Green Careers

Check out some of these careers in the renewable energy field!

## Engineers

Engineers are people who design and build new products, such as solar bike paths, solar tracking devices, floating solar panels, and much more. Engineers are problem solvers. A current challenge in creating solar panels is to design them so that they can hold the weight of humans, cars, and bikes without breaking. This would enable us to have solar sidewalks or roads!

## Installers and Technicians

Two of the most important jobs in the solar industry are solar installers and technicians. Solar installers are the people who attach solar panels to roofs or set up a solar farm on the ground. Solar installers make sure that the panels are installed in the right locations, sit at the correct angle, and will remain safely secure. Businesses around the country specialize in solar installations. Technicians are people who help monitor and repair solar systems once they are put in place.

## Researchers

Research jobs are key in the development of solar technology and other renewables. Researchers investigate problems using data. Solar researchers may study solar cells, photons, and materials used to make solar panels. Remember, we are still trying to create that super-efficient solar panel.

## Green Businesspeople

Are you interested in helping the solar industry grow? You might become a real estate agent, finance manager, project manager, or marketer for solar companies. All these jobs have roles to play in helping people use solar. Real estate agents can help people learn about the value of a house or business with solar panels. Finance managers help companies get loans to install and maintain solar farms. Project managers work with a team of engineers to complete projects. Marketers are needed to help solar companies sell their products.

# RENEWABLE ENERGY

**WORDS TO KNOW**

**agrivoltaics:** the use of land for both solar power generation and agricultural use.

**pollinator:** an insect or other animal that transfers pollen from the male part of a flower to the female part of a flower. Pollen is a fine, yellow powder produced by flowering plants that is needed by a flower to make a seed.

First, solar energy can be unpredictable. Although we can forecast weather, we can never be entirely certain what tomorrow's weather will be. If it is excessively cloudy or foggy, that reduces the amount of energy that solar panels produce.

On cloudy days, solar panels still generate power, but less of it. What if it's cloudy for an entire week? Solar technology may not produce enough energy when we need it. We need ways to store solar energy for whenever the sun doesn't shine, such as on cloudy days and during the night.

Storage of solar-generated energy is typically done with batteries and this continues to be a challenge. This is an area engineers are working hard to improve.

**Agrivoltaics** is a special way of using **land to grow crops and produce energy** from the sun at the same time. It helps encourage the use of land for **native vegetation and pollinators.**

An agrivoltaic farm combines land use for growing crops and providing space for solar panels.

Where we find solar energy is also an important consideration. Can you guess which areas have the most predictable weather for solar energy? If you guessed desert regions, you're right! A desert has less rain and less cloud cover. That makes America's Desert Southwest an incredible area for producing solar power.

Solar farms require large areas of land to produce enough energy to power cities and towns. Today, scientists and farmers are working together to combine land and solar in areas known as agrivoltaic. Many of these farms have raised solar panels with plants growing underneath them. The panels are tilted at an optimal angle to allow just enough sunlight for the plants. The solar panels are arranged a few feet apart to provide additional sunlight and space for farming equipment.

In the average home, 75 percent **of the electricity used to power** home electronics is consumed while the products are turned off! Idle power **consumes more electricity than all** the solar panels in America produce.

The metals required to build photovoltaic cells and batteries are something else we need to consider. Solar panels use silicon, silver, aluminum, and copper. Drilling and digging for metals negatively impacts the land, communities, and workers. The demand for minerals in solar must be met with environmental standards for both the workers and the places they come from.

And what happens to solar panels that are old and need to be scrapped? Can the materials be recycled? Yes, many parts of solar panels can now be recycled. On average, a solar panel has a life of about 30 years.

What do you think? Is solar power worth the tradeoff?

Let's explore another renewable energy that has the potential to change the way we treat our planet—wind!

## ESSENTIAL QUESTION

How can we use the sun to produce energy here on Earth?

# SEEING
# THE LIGHT

Most of the light that reaches Earth from space comes from the sun. Light that comes from the sun is called white light, although it is really a combination of all colors. As the sun sets, it sinks lower in the sky, which means that the sunlight must pass through more air in the atmosphere to reach your eyes. This gives blue light more time to be scattered away through the atmosphere. The remaining wavelengths that you can see are longer ones that get less scattered, such as orange and red—and this makes a sunset! Small particles in the air enhance the scattering effect, which is why, on hazy days, a sunset appears even redder. Want to see for yourself?

> Fill your glass all the way up with tap water.

> **Shine your flashlight through the glass of water from the side.** What color is the water? If you look at the glass from the front, what does it look like? Can you see the light traveling through the water? Is the light beam narrow or wide? Write down your observations in your science journal.

## Try This!

What happens if you replace the milk with other substances? Try it and find out!

> **Add about one teaspoon of milk to the water and stir until it's mixed.** How does the water look now? Is it still clear or does it look cloudy?

> **Shine the flashlight through the solution from the side.** Does the solution change color? Why? What color do you see? Can you still see the light traveling through the solution?

> **Shine the flashlight from the top of the glass.** What changes? Why?

## THINK ABOUT IT!
What's happening to the light waves as they pass through the water? Through the milk?

# CREATE A
# LIGHT BOX

Solid objects absorb light when it hits them, while water in bottles refracts light by bending it in different directions. Let's learn more about how light behaves with a light box!

> **Fill the plastic bottles with water.** Add food coloring to some of them.

> **Cover the top of the box with aluminum foil to help reflect light into the bottles.** Trace the bottom of the bottles on the top of the box and cut out the traced holes.

> **Cut a window in the side of the box.** It should be just big enough to peek inside.

> **Insert the bottles halfway into the holes.** Make sure enough of each bottle is still above the box for light to hit the bottles. Secure each bottle with tape.

> **Look through your observation hole.** What do you see inside the box? Write your observations in your science journal.

## Try This!

Use paper cups to cover the tops of some bottles to block the light. How does that change the pattern you see inside the box? How can this kind of solar technology be used in places with lots of sun but little access to power?

TEXT TO **WORLD**

Do you have solar power in your home? If so, where are your solar panels located? What do they provide energy for?

# MAKE A
# SOLAR OVEN

**Can you cook a marshmallow using the power of solar energy? Build a solar oven and find out!**

> **Remove one side of the box to create an opening.** If you're using a pizza box, you can simply cut a square out of the top.

> **Line the inside of the box with aluminum foil, shiny side facing in.** This will help reflect and concentrate the sunlight.

> **Tape black construction paper to the bottom of the box.** This is to absorb heat.

> **Cover the opening with plastic wrap.** Secure it tightly with tape to create a transparent window.

> **Set up your solar oven.** Choose a spot with direct sunlight.

> **Time to cook!** Place a marshmallow on a small dish inside the oven.

> **Use a thermometer to measure the initial temperature inside the oven.** Record the temperature in your science journal.

> **Close the oven.** Check the temperature at 10-minute intervals and record. How quickly does the temperature rise? What's happening to your marshmallow?

## Try This!

Try cooking or heating up other kinds of food, such as a grilled cheese sandwich or a bowl of soup. What happens? Can you think of ways to make your solar oven more efficient?

# Chapter 2

# CATCHING
# THE WIND

**There's nothing like a cool breeze on a hot summer day! And that breeze is good for more than just cooling you off. More than half the countries around the world use wind power!**

**ESSENTIAL QUESTION**

Why can wind be considered another form of solar energy?

In fact, wind is the largest source of renewable energy in the United States. Wind provides nearly 10.2 percent of the country's electricity, powering more than 40 million homes in America. That is equivalent to burning 760 million barrels of oil every year.

# RENEWABLE ENERGY

Wind energy relies on height. The higher a wind turbine is off the ground, the more energy it produces. The average wind turbine is 260 feet tall, which is three times taller than an average oak tree.

Building taller wind turbines is a challenge. It requires the **collaboration** of scientists and engineers from around the world.

The world's tallest wind turbine **is found near Stuttgart, Germany.** It's 808 feet!

As you watch the exciting development in the construction of wind turbines, keep in mind that wind is everywhere. It is found in all 50 states of the United States. Wind is also found in every country around the globe. There's plenty of it!

### Why Does the Wind Blow?

You can thank the sun! Wind is the movement of air, caused by the uneven heating of the earth by the sun and the earth's own **rotation**. Winds range from light breezes to natural hazards such as hurricanes and tornadoes. How does the sun create wind?

**Watch this video from the National Oceanic and Atmospheric Administration (NOAA) to learn more.**

🔎 NOAA SciJinks wind

## WHAT IS WIND?

Wind is air in motion. It's created by the sun heating the planet unevenly—as one area warms, another cools. The sun heats the air over land more quickly than it heats air over the ocean. As air warms, it **expands**. Warm air is less **dense** than cold air, and because warm air is less dense, it rises.

Take a look at this video about **early wind power.** How have **windmills** changed since early times?

🔎 Energy 101: Wind Power

This is how hot air balloons work! As the balloon fills with hot air, the area inside the balloon becomes less dense and rises above the heavier, colder air around it.

When warm air rises from the surface of the earth, it leaves what's called low **atmospheric pressure**. The cooler air from over the ocean, where there's high atmospheric pressure, rushes in to try and balance the pressure. We feel this **convection current** as wind!

## WORDS TO KNOW

**equator:** an imaginary line around the earth, halfway between the North and South Poles.

**anemometer:** a device that measures wind speed and pressure.

**trade winds:** winds that blow almost continually toward the equator from the northeast north of the equator and from the southeast south of the equator.

**jet stream:** a band of strong wind that blows from west to east across the globe.

This movement of warm air and cool air is what makes the wind blow. Predictable differences in temperature at the surface of Earth cause predictable global wind patterns.

As you can imagine, some parts of the earth are warmer than others. If you live near the **equator**, you receive more direct sun rays than any other place on Earth. Farther north and south of the equator, the sun warms the surface less. The air over deserts gets warmer than the air in the mountains. During the day, the air over the land usually gets warmer than the air over the water. At night, the opposite is true.

An **anemometer** is an instrument used to measure the speed of the wind. The number of times the device spins is calculated and converted into miles per hour.

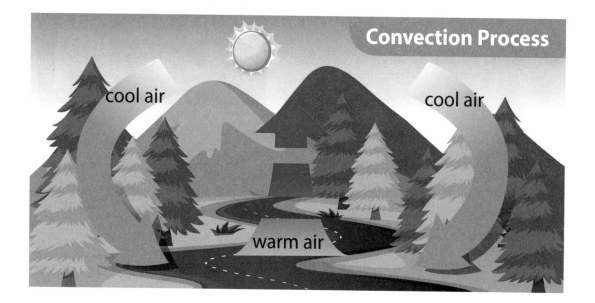

## Convection Process

cool air

cool air

warm air

Global wind patterns

Because we know where and when temperatures are going to rise and fall, we can predict where and when wind is going to happen. These winds are often grouped together as **trade winds**, easterlies, and westerlies.

## WHERE CAN WE FIND WIND?

You might notice that different areas of your town or city absorb more solar energy than others. Light-colored surfaces and water reflect more sunlight than dark surfaces, so those areas are cooler.

### Follow the Jet Stream!

**Jet streams** are narrow bands of strong wind that generally blow from west to east across the globe. Jet streams are located about 5 to 9 miles above Earth's surface. Earth has four primary jet streams. Jet streams can even make airplane trips shorter! If an airplane flies in a powerful jet stream generally from west to east it can get a boost, making the trip faster than an airplane traveling the same route east to west.

**Learn about the jet streams on Earth by watching this video.**

ρ NOAA jet stream

# RENEWABLE ENERGY

**Great Plains:** a large area of flat grassland in the center of the United States between the Mississippi River and the Rocky Mountains. Another word for this grassland is prairie.

Snow and ice reflect sunlight, too. Some types of land absorb more solar energy than others. Buildings and roads usually absorb more energy than lakes and oceans.

The sun's heat can cause wind patterns even at the local level.

Some places have more wind than others. The air over land usually gets warmer than the air over water.

When warm air rises and cool air takes its place, it gets windy. As long as the sun shines, there will be wind on Earth! The windiest areas in the United States are in the **Great Plains**, from Nebraska to Iowa. Texas is the state leader in providing wind power in the United States.

The largest wind turbine in the world **is in China! It stands 500 feet tall and has** blades the length of a football field!

## WINDMILL TO WIND TURBINE

How do we turn wind into energy? People have been harnessing the energy of the wind for about 4,000 years. Windmills were used to grind grain and pump water from the Middle East to China.

Early American farmers and colonists used windmills to grind wheat and corn, pump water, and cut wood at sawmills.

A wind farm is a group of three or more wind turbines **used to produce large** amounts of electricity.

Then, in Europe, people added big spinning arms to do even more work. In the 1800s, people such as James Blyth (1839–1906) in Scotland and others in America figured out how to use the wind to make electricity. They built special machines called wind turbines.

The ruins of a traditional windmill in Greece

39

**shaft:** a bar that connects gears and transfers power from one gear to another.

**generator:** a machine that converts mechanical energy into electricity.

**direct relationship:** a relationship where both variables increase or decrease together.

**inverse relationship:** a relationship where one variable increases as the other decreases.

**horizontal axis of rotation:** the movement of wind horizontally (from side to side) across the blades of a turbine.

**vertical axis of rotation:** the movement of wind vertically (up and down) across the blades of a turbine.

A wind turbine consists of four main parts—the tower, blades, **shaft**, and **generator**. A wind turbine can have as many as 8,000 parts. The largest turbine's blades cover an area equal to four of the world's largest passenger planes.

The tower holds the blades and enables them to access the wind high up in the sky. When the wind blows, it pushes against the blades of the wind turbines, causing them to spin around.

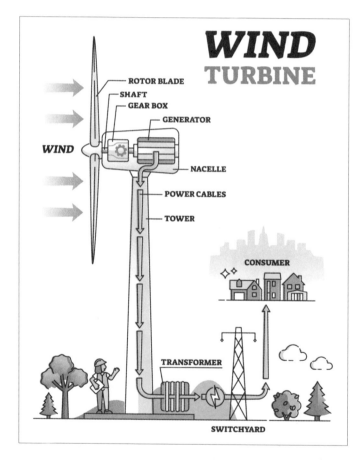

When the blades start turning, they move at 6 to 9 mph. And the higher the tower, the stronger the wind and the faster the blades can turn! Wind turbine blades can spin as fast as 180 mph in a strong wind.

As the blades spin, they cause a giant magnet in the shaft of the turbine to spin. The shaft is a bar that connects one gear to another and transfers power from one gear to another. The spinning magnet is surrounded by copper wire, and that's what generates electricity.

## DESIGNING WIND TURBINES

Wind turbines that generate electricity have changed a lot through time. One of the biggest changes has been the size and design of the blades. Longer blades produce more electricity, but as the blades get longer, the tower must get higher. This is called a **direct relationship**. As one increases, the other must also increase.

**The average wind turbine generates enough electricity in 46 minutes to power the average home in the United States for one month. That's a lot of power!**

As blades get bigger and towers get taller, the cost to generate electricity falls. This is called an **inverse relationship**.

Wind turbines come in many different designs, but all of them fall into one of two categories—**horizontal axis of rotation** or **vertical axis of rotation**.

A vertical axis wind turbine

Credit: Dwight Burdette (CC By 3.0)

## Water Conservation

Traditional power plants use a lot of water to produce the steam needed to generate electricity, but power plants using wind don't need water. The wind turns the blades of the turbine, not steam. This means wind energy helps to conserve water resources. Mathematicians predict that by the year 2050, using wind energy can save 260 billion gallons of water. That amount of water could fill 400,000 Olympic-size swimming pools.

## WORDS TO KNOW

**archaeological:** having to do with archaeology, the study of ancient people through the objects they left behind.

**river delta:** a collection of rocks and soil at the mouth of a river.

**onshore:** describes a wind farm that is built on land.

**offshore:** describes a wind farm that is built in the ocean, either attached on the ocean floor or floating on the water.

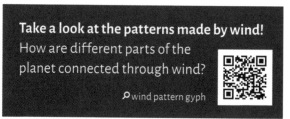

Take a look at the patterns made by wind! How are different parts of the planet connected through wind?

🔍 wind pattern gyph

A horizontal axis wind turbine is the more traditional design, and it looks like a large propeller. A vertical axis wind turbine is more useful in urban and low-lying areas where the direction of the wind frequently changes. The blades spin around like a carousel at the amusement park.

Today, wind-powered generators come in every size, from small turbines for individual homes to large wind farms that provide electricity for entire cities, and even countries. Both large and small wind turbines are cost effective and give off no pollution, other than that created during manufacture.

## Offshore Controversy

Off the coast of Martha's Vineyard, Massachusetts, a proposed wind farm is causing controversy. Objectors claim the company building the wind farm didn't do enough research into how it will affect marine life. Fishermen are concerned that their livelihoods will be interrupted. How can we make sure we are creating a greener future while still taking care of the people and animals at risk from new technologies?

## FARMING THE WIND

Humans have been farming for more than 12,000 years. **Archaeological** records suggest that the first example of farming was in the Tigris-Euphrates **river delta**. This is in modern-day Iraq. Archaeologists have found examples of farming on every continent and in all types of environments. Farming is important for food and jobs around the world.

This onshore wind farm in Oregon is growing! You can see a turbine under construction.

Credit: Tedder (CC BY 3.0)

On April 17, 1980, a new type of farming came to be—wind farming!

This was when the first wind farm in the United States was developed by the U.S. Department of Energy and NASA. A wind farm, or wind park, is a group of wind turbines installed in the same location and used to produce electricity. The first was located on the shoulder of Crotched Mountain in southern New Hampshire. There were 20 wind turbines.

Wind farms can be **onshore** or **offshore** farms. Onshore wind farms are placed solidly on dry ground. Offshore wind turbines are anchored directly to the ocean floor or float above the ocean floor.

**Wind farmers plant giant wind turbines just as agriculture farmers plant rows of corn.**

# RENEWABLE ENERGY

A large wind farm might consist of several hundred individual wind turbines and cover hundreds of square miles. The land between the turbines can still be used for agricultural or other purposes.

Wind farms generate so much electricity that they can power entire cities. They can connect directly to the **smart grid**, an electrical network that uses digital technology to allow renewable energy to be distributed to homes and businesses.

Since that first wind farm was created in 1980, more than 1,000 wind farm projects have been built in the world, with more than 71,000 individual wind turbines in the United States.

Micro-windmills are the size of a grain of rice. **They can be used to power small objects such as** smartphones and clocks. Micro-windmills are being built at the University of Texas at Arlington.

Eight of the 10 largest wind farms in the world are operated in America. The Alta Wind Energy Center in California is the largest wind farm in the United States, with the capacity to produce 1,320 MWs of power—enough electricity to power a million homes. Texas has another five of the largest wind farms. The U.S. Department of Energy estimates that wind power in the United States could provide enough electricity to meet 30 percent of all the country's electricity needs by 2050.

Wind power delivers public health and environmental benefits, too. These include reduced greenhouse gas emissions, reduced air pollutants, and reduced water consumption. Wind technology provides a local, sustainable, and essentially pollution-free electricity resource.

What happens when the wind doesn't blow? Engineers are working to improve energy storage systems, so we don't always need the wind to blow to benefit from wind energy.

## Green Careers

Take a look at these green jobs!

### Manufacturers

Factories that once created the steel, nails, and bolts for our railroads are now creating wind turbine parts. From the rotor blades to the towers and gearboxes, many parts are needed to make a wind turbine work. In the United States, more than 500 wind-related manufacturing facilities are found across 43 states. Manufacturing wind turbine parts is an important job if we are going to use wind to power our lives. GE Energy is the largest wind turbine manufacturer in the United States.

### Project Managers

Project managers work hand in hand with wind energy engineers to identify sites for wind turbines and manage business opportunities for wind energy. Wind project managers often must deal with environmental regulations and permits as well as conduct research. These activities must take place before wind energy installations can be built. Engineers help design and prepare the new sites for wind farms.

## WIND ENERGY TRADEOFFS

Wind power, like solar power, can be unpredictable. This is one reason towns and cities don't run on just solar power or just wind power. Our lives require a predictable supply of energy from multiple sources!

One of the major tradeoffs for wind energy is the impact wind turbines have on migrating birds. Because wind turbines can spin at more than 200 miles per hour at the tips of the blades—faster than many race cars—birds that fly near them are in danger of being struck.

### Windy Schools

Towns County Schools in Hiawassee, Georgia, are using a wind turbine to power the school campus. The school campus has an elementary, middle, and high school, all powered by wind! From K–12 schools to museums and community colleges, wind projects are being used across the country.

 Use this interactive map to find out where other wind energy projects are happening in the United States. Where is the closest one to your town?

🔍 wind energy products map

Although we don't know the exact number of birds that are injured or killed every year by wind turbines, we know the wind turbines have a negative impact on birds.

Another issue with wind turbines is that some people feel they spoil the scenic beauty of the landscape. Of course, beauty is in the eye of the beholder: One person may see a wind turbine as an eyesore, while another person may see turbines as graceful and a beautiful sign of progress and clean energy.

Wind turbines can create a whooshing noise when spinning. People who live near wind turbines can be impacted by the constant sound. Would you want to live near a turbine if it was always making a whooshing sound?

**Professor Paul Sclavounos, a professor of mechanical engineering and naval architecture, calculated it would take nearly 4,000 five-MW turbines, which would take up about 40-by-40 square miles, to power New York City.**

Despite these issues, wind technology provides a domestic, sustainable, and essentially pollution-free electricity resource. Researchers are working to make them better for birds and humans.

Using a combination of renewable energy sources ensures that one source will always work, even if the wind isn't blowing or the sun isn't shining. We need to use a variety of sources that complement each other. Let's check out how water power uses turbines in our next chapter.

## College Education

Kirkwood Community College in Iowa has a three-blade wind turbine. Each blade weighs up to 30,000 pounds. The power from the turbine is sold to the local utility company, which provides about $300,000 a year for the college. The wind turbine is being used as a living-learning laboratory for students who are studying energy production and distribution technologies.

**ESSENTIAL QUESTION**

Why can wind be considered another form of solar energy?

# WIND
# CAN DO WORK

**Use your engineering skills to design a windmill, then test how powerful the wind can be!**

❯ **Turn the cup upside down.** Using a ruler, cut the wide straw to 3 inches in length.

❯ **Tape the straw horizontally on top of the cup.** There should be an equal amount of straw on both sides.

❯ **Use the windmill blade template to make your windmill blades.** You can find the template at nomadpress.net/templates.

❯ **Measure a half inch from the end of the narrow straw.** Make a mark.

❯ **Insert a pin through the narrow straw at this mark.** This is the front of the straw.

❯ **Slide the narrow straw through the windmill blades until the back of the blades rest against the pin.** Gently slide each blade over the end of the straw. Secure the blades to the straw using tape.

❯ **Insert the narrow straw into the wider straw on the cup.** Tape the string to the end of the small straw. Tie the other end of the string to a paper clip, making sure you have 12 inches of string from the straw to the top of the paper clip.

❯ **On the very end of the narrow straw, near where the string is attached, fasten a binder clip in place.** This is for balance and to keep the string from winding around the straw.

## TOOL KIT

- large foam cup
- ruler
- scissors
- extra-wide straw
- masking tape
- 4-blade windmill template
- narrow straw
- 2 straight pins
- string or thread
- paper clips
- binder clip
- fan
- marker
- science journal

Many of the components of wind turbines installed in the United States are manufactured here, with more than 500 wind-related manufacturing facilities across the country. The U.S. wind industry currently employs more than 125,000 people, including 23,543 in manufacturing and 45,088 in construction.

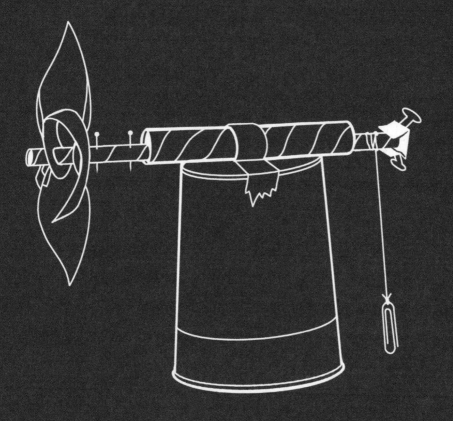

> **Slide the narrow straw forward to bring the binder clip next to the wider straw.** Place a second straight pin through the narrow straw at the other end of the wider straw. This will keep the blades away from the cup while still allowing them to move and spin.

> **Place your windmill in front of the fan.** How does it work? Is there anything you can do to improve the design? Record your observations in your science journal.

## Try This!

If you had to redesign your blades, what would you do differently? Why? Redesign your blades. What shapes work best? What else can you use to attach the parts to one another? Test your new designs. Note your observations and compare the designs in your science journal.

### TEXT TO **WORLD**

Have you ever seen a wind farm? Do you think it looks beautiful or ugly?

# WIND
# VANE

There are two main measurements to describe wind: direction and speed. Wind direction is described by using the direction that the wind came from. For example, a southerly wind would blow from the south to the north. Wind direction is measured in a number of ways, including with weathervanes, flags, and windsocks. In this activity, you will create a wind vane (also known as a weathervane) that shows the direction of the wind. Finding the direction of the prevailing wind is an important part of knowing where to build wind farms.

> **Draw a block arrow and a rectangle on the cardboard.** Cut out both shapes. The arrow needs to be a little bigger than the rectangle to ensure it is pushed by the wind. Tape or glue the shapes onto each end of the straw.

> **Roll the playdough into a ball.** Push the pencil tip into the playdough so it stands vertically.

> **Push the pin through the straw into the eraser.** Make sure the straw can spin around freely.

> **Choose a spot outside that isn't sheltered from the wind and watch as the wind vane spins.** Which way is the wind blowing?

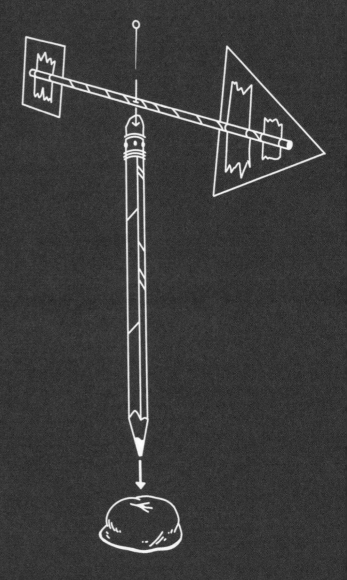

## Try This!

Use a compass to see which direction the wind is blowing from. Check the direction of the wind every day for a month and record your observations in your journal. Where would you build a wind turbine?

# Chapter 3

# THE
# POWER OF H$_2$O

THERE REALLY ARE A LOT OF RENEWABLE ENERGY OPTIONS OUT THERE.

IT'S AWESOME THAT OUR CITY USES SO MANY OF THEM TO PRODUCE OUR ENERGY, TOO!

AND EVERY YEAR THEY GET MORE EFFICIENT!

Water is one of our most important resources. We use water every day to wash, cook with, and drink. The ocean provides food, medicines, **minerals**, and energy resources. Water supports jobs, tourism, farming, and, of course, swimming! We use water to move **goods** from one place to another. Plus, we use water to grind grain, grow **crops**, and generate electricity.

Water is constantly moving. Think about all the different sources of water—oceans, lakes, rivers, the creek behind your backyard, and even that **glacier** you might have seen on television. All this water moves. Sometimes, water moves because of **gravity** and currents. Think of a river or stream. Water also moves through **evaporation**.

**ESSENTIAL QUESTION**

How does water generate electricity?

# RENEWABLE ENERGY

## WORDS TO KNOW

**mineral:** a solid, nonliving substance found in the earth and in water, such as gold, salt, or copper.

**goods:** things made or grown that can be bought, sold, or traded.

**crops:** plants grown for food and other uses.

**glacier:** a sheet of ice that slowly moves downhill due to gravity.

**gravity:** a force that pulls objects to the earth.

**evaporation:** the process by which a liquid becomes a gas.

**hydrokinetic:** related to the motion of fluids.

**marine:** found in the ocean or having to do with the ocean.

It's easy to picture rivers moving, but what about glaciers? How do they move? Glaciers are slow-moving rivers of ice. You usually can't see them move just by watching them, but if you measure their progress during a long period of time, you can tell they are moving.

The energy of moving water is called **hydrokinetic** energy. The power that results from hydrokinetic energy is called hydropower. It is the most widely used form of renewable energy in the world. Hydropower accounts for more than 50 percent of the electricity generated from a renewable source. Hydropower is produced in 150 countries and is one of the oldest power sources on the planet.

The Nigardsbreen glacier in Norway moves slowly, though sometimes the ice melts enough so large chunks break off, which can be hazardous.

**From outer space, our planet looks like a blue marble. Nearly 71 percent of the surface of Earth is covered in water.**

This image of Earth taken by astronauts aboard *Apollo 17* in 1972 shows how much water covers the surface of the planet.
Credit: NASA

In this chapter, we will explore how we use the power of water to generate electricity. Both old and new inventions help us convert the energy from water into energy we can use to do other things.

The earth's waterways are not only home to many **marine** species, they also provide food and medicines for many communities. Waterways can be used as a highway for transportation of goods and people and play a role in supporting local economies.

Humans have been harnessing the power of water for thousands of years. The Greeks used water wheels for grinding wheat into flour more than 2,000 years ago. In the 1080s in England, there were more than 5,600 water wheels being used in 3,000 different locations. By the late tenth century, the Chinese government owned many water mills to supply the capital with ground flour.

## MODERN HYDROPOWER

The evolution of modern hydropower began in the mid-1700s with the invention of the turbine. You learned in the last chapter that turbines are key to generating electricity from wind. They are also needed for creating electricity from the movement of water.

Hydropower has seen several advancements in the past 150 years. This includes the creation of **hydroelectric power plants**.

A typical hydroelectric plant is a system with three parts: a power plant, a **dam**, and a reservoir. The water behind the dam flows through an intake and pushes against blades in a turbine, causing them to turn. The turbine spins a generator to produce electricity. Transmission lines carry power from the plant to our homes and towns.

The first hydroelectric power plant in the United States opened on the Fox River near Appleton, Wisconsin, on September 30, 1882. Since that time, we have relied mostly on dams in rivers to create hydropower. Today, one of the oldest hydroelectric power plants still operates—it's been turning since 1891 in Whiting, Wisconsin!

The Itaipu Plant situated on the Paraná River between Brazil and Paraguay produces the greatest amount of electricity annually—14,000 MWs!

The first water turbine was created in 1880. It was used **to make an electric spark to provide light for a theater** and storefront in Grand Rapids, Michigan. In 1881, a water turbine in a flour mill provided street **lighting in Niagara Falls, New York.**

Learn how hydropower works in this video. How are wind and hydropower similar?

Energy 101: Hydropower

## POWERFUL DAMS

Dams are one of the oldest technologies created by humans to harness hydrokinetic energy. Dams store energy for later use by holding back vast amounts of water. Interestingly, most dams in the United States were constructed for **irrigation** and flood control. Only a small number of dams are used to produce electricity.

In the United States, we produce clean, renewable electricity from roughly 2,500 dams. Most dams are found on rivers. We also have more than 80,000 non-powered dams, or dams that do not produce electricity at all. When people think of hydropower and dams, they might imagine structures such as the Hoover Dam on the Arizona-Nevada border or the Glen Canyon Dam in Arizona.

**Hydropower is the main renewable energy source the United States relies on—more than wind, solar, or geothermal power.**

As energy is needed, water is released to flow through a turbine to generate electricity. The amount of electricity that can be generated depends on how far the water drops and how much water moves through the system. The electricity can be transported through long-distance electric lines to homes, factories, and businesses.

Inside the Itaipu Plant
Credit: Martin St-Amant (CC By 3.0)

# RENEWABLE ENERGY

China, Brazil, Canada, the United States, and Russia are the five largest producers of hydropower. More than 1 million people get electricity from the Hoover Dam in Nevada!

The Three Gorges Dam on the Yangtze River in China is the largest in the world. This dam produces 20 times more electricity than the Hoover Dam.

Why would engineers build a dam if it does not produce electricity? What other uses can dams provide? Dams can be used to help store water for irrigation, create new lakes for recreational purposes, and control flooding on rivers. Using new, modern technology, many of America's 80,000 non-powered dams could be converted into energy-producing facilities.

The Three Gorges Dam in China

Credit: Le Grand Portage, Rehman (CC BY 2.0)

## PUMP STORAGE

What do engineers do when they generate lots of extra electricity? In the past, if you didn't use the electricity you produced from renewable energy sources, you'd lose it. What a waste! To save this precious energy from escaping dams, engineers came up with **pump storage**.

When a hydropower plant produces more energy than is being consumed, engineers use the extra energy to pump water uphill into a **reservoir**. Here, the water waits. Later, when the energy is needed, the water is allowed to flow back downhill through a turbine, producing electricity.

## PUMPED HYDROPOWER STORAGE

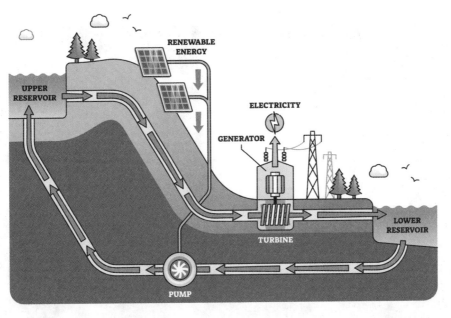

Pump storage of water is a critical part of our renewable energy future. And in areas where there's lots of sun and wind, those renewable energies can be used to pump water from the lower reservoir to the higher one to be stored for later use.

## WORDS TO KNOW

**tide:** the daily rising and falling of ocean water, based on the pull of the moon's and sun's gravity.

**gravitational effect:** the force of attraction between two masses.

**tidal power:** another form of hydropower, using tides.

**super magnet:** the strongest type of permanent magnets ever made.

**kinetic energy:** energy created from motion.

Pumping technology makes sure that the extra energy we harness on very sunny or windy days can be stored and used when needed.

## THE FORCE BEHIND THE TIDES

Have you ever spent the day at the beach and noticed the sandy parts get wider and narrower if you're there for several hours? These changes to the beach are the result of low **tides** and high tides that take place every 12 hours and 52 minutes on Earth. Tides play a major role in hydropower.

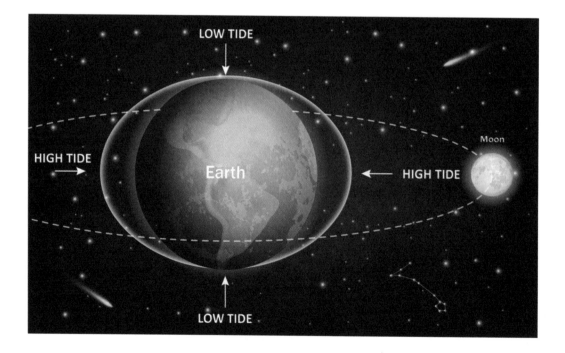

The moon, sun, and Earth's rotation are responsible for tides. Because the moon is so close to the sun—only 250,000 miles away—it has a larger **gravitational effect** on Earth than the sun.

On the side of the planet facing the moon, water bulges because the moon's gravity is pulling on it. On the side of the planet facing away from the moon, water bulges because as the moon's gravity pulls on Earth, the water on the far side is left with less pull. These bulges are high tides. What would happen to the tides on our planet if the moon suddenly disappeared?

**Tidal power**, or tidal energy, is another form of hydropower that can be converted into electricity. Tidal power has incredible potential because tides are more predictable than wind energy and solar power.

The moon revolves around Earth every 27 days, 7 hours, **43 minutes, and 11.6 seconds. At the same time, the** earth spins all the way around each day. The moon's gravity causes water **to bulge on the near and far sides** of planet Earth.

Engineers have developed buoy systems made from **super magnets** that rise and fall with the tides and waves and generate electricity. Tidal generators make use of the **kinetic energy** of moving water to power turbines. Similar to wind turbines, tidal turbines use the flow of water caused by rising and falling tides to make their turbines spin.

The Pelamis P2 wave energy device

Credit: Scottish Government

## WORDS TO KNOW

**water cycle:** the natural recycling of water through evaporation, condensation, precipitation, and collection.

**water vapor:** the gas form of water in the air.

**condense:** when a gas cools down and changes into a liquid.

**precipitation:** condensed water vapor that falls to the earth's surface in the form of rain, snow, sleet, or hail.

**topsoil:** the upper layer of soil.

## SUN AND WATER

We know that the moon causes the tides. The sun also affects the tides, but to a much lesser extent since it's so far away. What other effect does the sun have on water? The sun is responsible for the **water cycle**!

The water cycle causes rain and snow. Rain and snowfall replenish our rivers, lakes, and mountain snowpack. Without the water cycle, these would all run dry. Without the water cycle, all water would end up in the oceans and never return to land. And we wouldn't have any hydropower!

Water always flows downhill because of gravity. How does the water get back up to the top of the hill? How do streams stay full if water is constantly flowing down? Water in the ocean evaporates and becomes **water vapor** in the atmosphere. Eventually, this water vapor **condenses** into clouds and falls back to Earth in the form of **precipitation**—rain or snow. It flows back to the rivers and eventually to the ocean. A drop of water in the ocean can take anywhere from a day to 3,000 years to evaporate and fall back to Earth as rain.

**Everything we make requires the use of water. It takes about 5,200 cubic feet of water to produce a new car. This includes the making of its tires.**

## Life on Mars?

As far as we know, Earth is the only planet in our solar system whose surface always has liquid water on it. This liquid water supports life on Earth. Solid water is known to exist on the moon, deep in craters, and underground. Scientists exploring Mars have discovered evidence of flowing water just under the surface. This means there could have been life forms on those celestial bodies.

Without the water cycle, we would live in a world without lakes, ponds, rivers, glaciers, and snow, and we wouldn't have any need for dams. What else would be missing from a world without the water cycle?

How do we know how much water there is on Earth? One way is by measuring the amount of water in the top two inches of soil everywhere on Earth's surface.

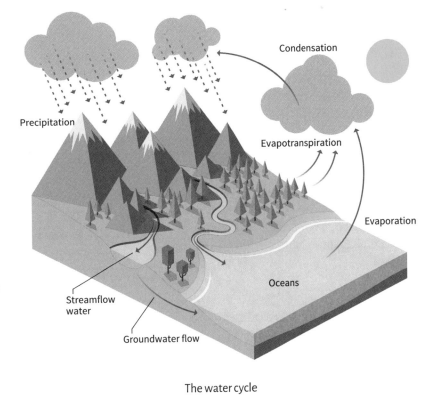

The water cycle

NASA's Soil Moisture Active Passive (SMAP) is a satellite in space that collects data on the amount of moisture in **topsoil**. The topsoil is where we grow food and where plants live.

SMAP is designed to measure soil moisture every two or three days during a three-year period. It gathers data every time the satellite loops around the world. This provides scientists with a steady stream of measurements of changes in soil moisture—month after month, season after season, year after year. The data helps us understand the movement of water on Earth.

**Check out the work of the scientists behind SMAP at this website!** Why is it important to have a constant stream of data year after year?

🔎 SMAP

# RENEWABLE ENERGY

## TRADEOFFS

Power from the movement of water is the most abundantly utilized source of renewable energy in the world. But what are the impacts of using water to generate electricity?

The use of dams is common around the world. Dams are used for irrigation, making electricity, gathering water, controlling flooding, and recreation. Dams stop the natural flow of rivers. The **spawning grounds** of certain species of fish have been completely cut off because of dams on rivers. River dams also change the **nutrients** that flow downstream. This change in nutrients can impact living things for up to a thousand miles away, even affecting the ocean **ecosystem** where rivers discharge.

Sometimes, people have to leave their homes to make way for a new dam. How might you feel if your family had to move because the land your house was on was needed for hydroelectricity?

62

You can see how the water level has changed in Lake Mead.

Countries are using new guidelines to help weigh the pros and cons of dam projects. Engineers think about the location, temperature, weather conditions, and depth of water when building a dam. The type of dam and the materials used to construct it affect the environment.

Guidelines from the World Commission on Dams provides a framework for governments to evaluate the social, environmental, political, and financial impacts of dam projects. This analysis helps countries determine if the benefits outweigh the environmental impacts.

If a person yelled for eight years, **seven months, and six days, they would** produce enough energy to heat one cup of coffee.

Climate change is also impacting our ability to rely on hydropower. Month to month and year to year, the amount of water available for hydropower systems can vary. Changes in weather, **droughts**, and precipitation levels disrupt electricity generation. Lake Mead, where the Hoover Dam sits, has lost hundreds of feet of water level in the past two decades as drought has plagued the region.

**aquatic:** related to water.

**corrode:** to rust, or wear away metal by a chemical reaction.

**oceanographer:** a scientist who studies the ocean.

**vent:** a hole that lets air escape. In nature, a vent is a crack in the earth's surface that lets hot gas escape.

**submersible:** a boat that can go below the surface of the water.

What happens if someday there isn't enough water in the reservoir for the dam to operate? Many countries are looking to pair hydropower with other renewable sources, such as wind and solar, to help meet energy demands.

Systems that capture the energy in the tides and currents of the oceans can affect **aquatic** ecosystems. From the material used to make the systems to their effects on the ocean floor, we are faced with some challenges in capturing the ocean's energy. Saltwater **corrodes** metal parts. Sea snakes, which are long mechanisms that collect energy generated from waves, might be hard for people on boats to see.

A sea snake or water turbine installation can disrupt the ocean floor. More research and new designs using different materials will help us capture the ocean's energy. Engineers are designing new technologies to solve many of the issues with hydroelectric tools.

## Deep Diver

Cindy Lee Van Dover (1954– ) is an **oceanographer** and explorer who studies the ecology of deep sea **vent** communities. Cindy was the first female pilot of *Alvin*, one of the world's first deep-ocean **submersibles**. She has led many *Alvin* expeditions to study deep sea vents and collect specimens for further study. In 1989, her work led to the discovery and characterization of a geothermal source of light at vents and investigations of its biological significance.

## Green Careers

The renewable energy industry needs a lot of people working together to make renewable energy affordable and easy for everyone to access!

### Hydrologists

Hydrologists help study the movement of water. They analyze soil, look at the physical properties of ground and surface waters, and study precipitation. Their work helps us understand the power of water. We can also learn new ways of protecting our water sources and everything that relies on that water.

Hydrologist Erin White takes high-precision water velocity measurements at Yellowstone National Park.

### Civil and Structural Engineers

Civil and structural engineers help design and find the best places for hydroelectric projects. Hydroelectric projects include the building of dams, reservoirs, and power plants. An important part of the work of civil and structural engineers is ensuring the safety of these projects once they are built.

### Environmental Scientists

Environmental scientists study the plants, animals, and water near hydroelectric projects. Monitoring the health of the water near these projects is important when projecting energy generation and the impact on wildlife that lives in the waters. These scientists collect data on water, oxygen, and temperature levels.

**The national database of the U.S. Army Corps of Engineers lists about 75,000 dams. You can see where they are on an online interactive map.** What parts of the country have the most dams? What parts have the least? Why?

PS

🔍 Army Corps Dam Map

**civilization:** a community of people that is advanced in art, science, and government.

**humid:** a weather condition marked by large amounts of water vapor in the atmosphere.

All these hydropower inventions show us how powerful water really is. Life on Earth is linked to water, and our existence is dependent on water. You could say that our whole **civilization** is built on the use of water.

Humans have been harnessing water to perform work for thousands of years. Yet, we have explored less than 20 percent of the oceans! Much is left to learn about the water that covers most of our planet. The oceans could help to cleanly power us into the next century and beyond.

The oceans have enough water to fill about 352,670 trillion gallon-size milk containers! **At any given moment, the atmosphere contains approximately 37.5** million billion gallons of water, or 37.5 quadrillion gallons.

The future of harnessing electricity from water is best paired with other renewable sources, such as wind and solar, so that we have reliable energy no matter what the weather is.

We must also continue to study and protect our water.

We've discussed solar, wind, and hydro energy. We also know how to harness the heat energy that comes from the center of our planet. We'll explore geothermal energy in the next chapter.

**ESSENTIAL QUESTION**

How does water generate electricity?

TEXT TO **WORLD**

Do you live near a river or ocean? What do you notice about the water?

# MAKE A
# RAIN GAUGE

**TOOL KIT**
- scissors
- empty jar or plastic bottle
- ruler
- permanent marker
- science journal

Scientists need to know how much water is in the ground. This information can help keep droughts and floods from occurring. It can also help scientists decide whether to build dams. Farmers find it useful to know rainfall amounts so they can provide extra water for their crops. One way you can measure the rain that falls in your yard is with a rain gauge!

**Have an adult help with the cutting!**

> Ask an adult to help you cut off the top the bottle.

> Lay the bottle flat and hold a ruler against the side. Mark every centimeter up the side.

> Stand the bottle outside in an open area. It should be away from any trees that might trap some of the rain.

> Monitor your rain gauge every day and record your findings in your science journal. Be sure to empty the water after you measure it every day!

On a hot, **humid day during the summer, you sweat a lot. Humidity is the** amount of water vapor in the air.

> Record your observations in your science journal. Even if your rain gauge has no water, enter zero—that's important data to have! How much water falls on average during a week? Add up the results for seven days and divide that number by 7 to get your average.

## THINK ABOUT IT!

In general, hydropower generation has a close relationship to precipitation. A drought will decrease power generation. An increase in precipitation will lead to an increase in power generation. Is your area in a drought?

# MAKE YOUR OWN
# DAM

## TOOL KIT

- small square plastic tub or aquarium
- measuring tape
- cardboard
- pencil
- clay
- cup
- water
- paper towels

Dams control the flow of water, create electricity with hydropower, and can be used for emergency water control. Construct this simple model to understand how a dam works when holding back water.

➤ **Measure the long way down the center line of the plastic tub.** You'll want to measure from one inside wall to the other with measuring tape.

➤ **On the cardboard, draw a straight line of the same length.**

➤ **Build a wall of clay along the drawn line.** The wall should be about 1 inch tall and the length of the line.

➤ **Set the wall inside the tub.** Adjust the length of the wall as needed to create a wall that fits very tightly into the tub.

➤ **Pour water slowly into one side of the tub.** What happens?

## Try This!

Various materials are used for dam construction, such as timber, rock, concrete, earth, steel, or a combination of these materials. Try building your dam using another material, such as rocks or a dry clay. What happens?

## Ocean Champion

Katsuko Saruhashi (1920–2007) is renowned for her groundbreaking research as a geochemist. A geochemist is a scientist who studies the chemical composition of and chemical changes in the solid matter of the earth. She was the first to accurately measure the concentration of carbonic acid in water, which has helped oceanographers. She also developed a technique to trace the travel of radioactive fallout across the oceans that led to restricting unsafe oceanic nuclear experimentation in 1963, which keeps marine life healthier.

# EXPERIENCE
# WATER PRESSURE

Water pressure is a key element in hydroelectric power. Try putting the pressure on yourself!

> **Caution: Have an adult help you heat the pushpin or thumbtack!**

> **Fill the 2-liter bottle with water.** Leave some space at the top for air.

> **Heat up the pushpin or thumbtack with a candle or lighter.** Ask an adult to help.

> **Hold the bottle over the container to collect water.** Carefully poke a small hole near the bottom of the bottle.

> **What happens?** How fast does the water come out? Which way does the stream go?

> **Make additional holes at different heights along the side of the bottle.** How does this change the flow of water? Draw your observations in your science journal.

**In Norway, 20 hydropower plants produce about 99 percent of the country's energy.**

## Try This!

With a new bottle, make smaller or larger holes and see how that affects the water pressure! What happens if you use a larger or smaller bottle?

# Chapter 4

## TAPPING INTO
# MOTHER EARTH

**Have you ever seen volcanoes or hot springs? These sites are evidence of the power of the energy beneath the ground!**

For thousands of years, people have known about the beauty and power of geothermal energy. Ancient Greeks believed in a pair of gods who presided over the **hot springs** and **geysers** in the region that is now known as Palaia in Sicily, Italy. Ancient Romans used geothermal water at Pompeii, Italy, to heat buildings. **Medieval** wars were fought over lands that contained hot springs.

**The deeper you go into planet Earth, the hotter the temperature.**

**ESSENTIAL QUESTION**

How can we use heat from inside Earth to power our lives on the surface of the planet?

## Old Faithful

One of the largest geysers is found in Yellowstone National Park in the United States. This geyser, named "Old Faithful," is capable of shooting 3,700 to 8,400 gallons of boiling water to an estimated height of 106 to 185 feet, lasting up to 5 minutes.

 **Wow! Take a look!**

🔍 Old Faithful video

**hot spring:** a natural pool of water heated by hot or molten rock. Hot springs are found in areas with active volcanoes.

**geyser:** a hot spring under pressure that shoots boiling water or steam into the air.

**medieval:** a period of time between the fall of the Roman Empire and the Renaissance, roughly between the years 350 and 1450. Also known as the Middle Ages.

# RENEWABLE ENERGY

In North America, archaeological evidence shows that the first human use of geothermal resources occurred more than 10,000 years ago. Native American tribes established their homes near volcanic hot springs. These springs served as sources of warmth, and their minerals were known to have healing powers.

Today, geothermal energy is at work in many countries, such as New Zealand, Kenya, El Salvador, and the Philippines. In Iceland, much of the country runs on geothermal energy. The United States is currently the leader in geothermal energy production, powering more than 4 million homes with clean, renewable, geothermal energy.

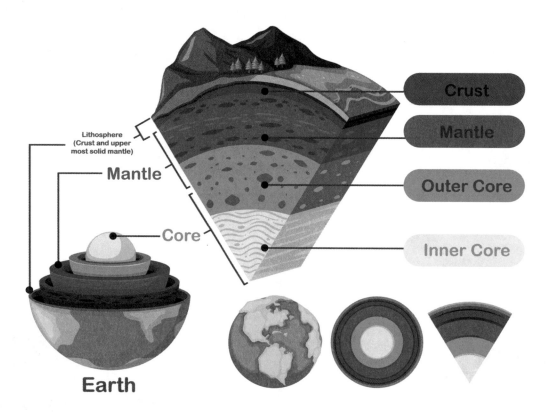

Lithosphere (Crust and upper most solid mantle)

Mantle

Core

Earth

Crust

Mantle

Outer Core

Inner Core

Geothermal energy is heat from far inside Earth. To get to this heat, we dig wells deep underground to connect to reservoirs of steam and hot water. This steam is used to generate electricity or to heat and cool buildings.

If we drill deep into Earth's crust, we can find enough thermal energy to power entire cities and towns. Engineers and scientists are working to design ways to use this energy to heat and cool buildings efficiently and generate clean electricity. To understand more about geothermal energy, let's dig deeper into our knowledge of Earth.

## HOW HOT?

Earth, just like humans and animals, has interacting parts. Imagine cutting Earth in half just as you might cut an apple. You would see three distinct layers: the **core**, the **mantle**, and the **crust**. These layers vary in thickness and temperature.

### On the Surface

We don't need to drill deeply to tap into geothermal energy. In fact, geothermal energy is released right at the surface of Earth in many places. Hot springs are natural pools of water that the heat of Earth has warmed up. Volcanoes are an example of geothermal energy escaping. Lava is rock that has melted and flowed out of volcanoes.

Look at this map to see all the places in the world with volcanoes.

**PS**

&#x1f50e; volcano discovery map

**PS** This map shows areas where hot springs are found in the United States. Do you notice anything about the areas that have the greatest number of hot springs? Most of the Earth's geothermal energy does not bubble out as magma, water, or steam.

&#x1f50e; NOAA thermal springs map

## WORDS TO KNOW

**continental crust:** Earth's crust on which land is found.

**oceanic crust:** Earth's crust that lies under the oceans.

**earthquake:** a sudden movement in the outer layer of Earth, which releases stress built up from the motion of Earth's plates.

**seismic:** related to earthquakes.

At the very center of Earth, in the inner core, scientists estimate the temperature is more than 10,000 degrees Fahrenheit (5,538 degrees Celsius). That is hot enough to melt solid iron! But because of the pressure from the rest of the planet, the core stays solid.

The "Ring of Fire" is a term given to **the circle shape of** volcanoes around the Pacific Ocean.

The mantle is also very hot, hotter than the surface of Venus. The temperature varies from 1,832 degrees Fahrenheit (1,000 degrees Celsius) near its boundary with the crust to 6,692 degrees Fahrenheit (3,700 degrees Celsius) near its boundary with the core. The crust gets colder the closer you get to the surface.

How thick is the skin of an apple? It is barely the width of a piece of paper! Similarly, Earth's crust is paper-thin when compared to the immense thickness of the planet. The crust is about 1 percent the thickness of Earth.

Where do you think Earth's crust is thickest? Where do you think it is thinnest? Earth's crust varies in thickness from mountaintops to the ocean floor. The thicker parts of the crust, called **continental crust**, are near mountains, such as the Himalayas and Andes. Here, the crust can be up to 40 miles thick. The thinnest parts of the crust are found under the ocean and are called **oceanic crust**. Many places on the ocean floor have a crust that is only 3 miles thick. That is about 352 school buses lined up.

Watch this video about the earth's layers and how they formed. How does Earth's position in space affect the renewable energies we have available to us?

Nat Geo Earth 101

**Earthquakes** and the **seismic** waves they give off let us gather data about the inside of Earth. This data tells us about our planet's inner temperatures and the thickness of the layers inside it.

The seismic data shows that Earth's inner and outer cores are about 2,100 miles thick. That is equal to 246,000 school buses lined up. Earth's mantle is 1,800 miles thick.

We might not always feel it, but the surface of the Earth is always releasing or holding heat. That means that in the winter, when it is cold outside, a few feet underground it remains warm. In the summer, when it is hot outside, a few feet underground you'll find cool dirt.

## CAPTURING THE HEAT

As you learned in previous chapters, energy is converted into electricity by getting a magnet inside a turbine to spin. How does geothermal energy get a turbine to spin? By using steam! Just as steam powered trains in the 1800s, steam from geothermal energy is now powering cities. Steam powered trains by converting its energy to mechanical energy, while geothermal steam usually has its energy converted to electrical energy.

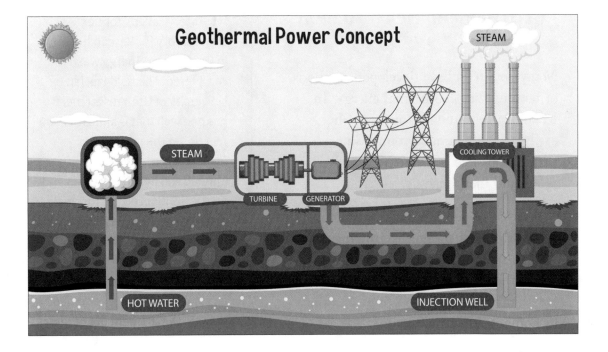

In a steam engine on a train, coal was burned to heat water. As the water boiled, it changed from a liquid to a gas, or steam. When forced into the engine of the train, the steam made the engine move. The pistons' movements caused the wheels of the train to spin.

With geothermal energy, we don't need to burn fossil fuels to create steam. Instead, hot rocks naturally change liquid water into steam. The steam's movement causes the blades of a turbine to spin and generate electricity. Hot stuff!

Beginning in 1892, America's first geothermal energy heating system powered Boise, Idaho. Today, nearly 450 homes are still powered in Boise by this plant. The first geothermal plant to generate electricity was built in California in 1921 and still operates today. This plant, known as Big Geysers plant, is part of the largest geothermal field in the world.

## GEOTHERMAL HEAT PUMPS

Many countries have developed methods of tapping into geothermal energy. In Iceland, the abundant sources of hot, easily accessible underground water make it possible to heat and cool homes safely and inexpensively.

The use of geothermal heat pumps for heating and cooling is growing in regions such as New England in the United States. Utilities and homeowners are working together to bring solutions to home heating and cooling.

## Dig Deep

In 2021, a first-of-its-kind field laboratory called Frontier Observatory for Research in Geothermal Energy was completed. The field lab, led by University of Utah researchers, has one well that is almost 11,000 feet under the ground and another is currently being dug. This lab will help us research and develop enhanced geothermal systems technologies. For example, scientists will be able to look at new ways to drill cheaply, test reservoirs, and conduct flow-tests. The laboratory is funded by the U.S. Department of Energy.

To use a geothermal heat pump, engineers drill about 10 to 300 feet into the ground to lay a pipe called a **slinky loop**. Water typically moves through the pipes, providing heat or cooling from deep inside the ground.

Some geothermal heat pumps can even supply a home with hot water for cooking and bathing. Geothermal heat pumps can provide a great way to cool and heat homes in many places around the world.

## FINDING THAT HEAT

Geothermal energy experts drill into Earth's crust with very large drills to find areas with the hottest temperatures. Have you ever seen a home power drill? How long is the longest drill bit? Most power drills have a drill bit that is at most a few inches long.

**Watch this video to learn more about how geothermal energy works!** How does geothermal fit into the family of renewable energies?

🔍 Energy 101: Geothermal Energy

Geothermal scientists use drills that are miles long. In fact, the deepest scientists have ever drilled into the ground is 40,230 feet, or 7.62 miles. That's a long drill bit!

The super-hot earth provides us with a chance to generate clean, renewable energy. This can support our society's demand for electricity without polluting. Geothermal is a strong, renewable source of electricity able to provide energy 24 hours a day without interruption.

## GEOTHERMAL ENERGY TRADEOFFS

Geothermal energy can produce a predictable, constant flow of energy. The problem with geothermal energy is the high cost of digging deep into the ground. It costs millions of dollars to drill a single geothermal energy well.

Geologists are working hard to identify geothermal sources to power our lives. But it is hard to be 100-percent right when looking for heat that can be used. Sometimes, a geothermal well is drilled that does not have enough heat to produce energy.

Look at this map showing areas in the United States where the temperatures of the rocks are warmer and cooler. Which region has the greatest potential for geothermal?

interactive geothermal map

## More Green Careers!

### Geothermal Technicians

Geothermal technicians are the experts you need at a geothermal power plant. These people monitor, control, and repair the devices that harness geothermal power. Many of them maintain geothermal heat pumps used to heat and cool buildings.

### Geothermal Scientists

Do you dig earth science? Earth science rocks! Jobs in research and development of geothermal technology may be the right fit for you. These roles in industry, national labs, and universities provide data and analysis to help us understand the power within Earth. Maybe you can help us locate that geothermal energy.

Geothermal electricity generation requires water or steam at high temperatures—300 to 700 degrees Fahrenheit (149 to 371 degrees Celsius). In addition, power plants need to be built near geothermal reservoirs. As with other renewable energies, this can limit where geothermal energy systems can be built. Today, only six states in the United States use geothermal energy to generate electricity.

The more you learn, the more you realize that Earth's ability to provide us with clean, renewable energy is amazing. The use of geothermal energy has been steadily growing since the 1970s. How far can we go using this renewable energy? That is up to the next generation of geothermal engineers.

We have one more renewable energy technology to explore. Buckle up, because this energy just might change how we power our cars!

**ESSENTIAL QUESTION**

How can we use heat from inside Earth to power our lives on the surface of the planet?

# VOLCANO!

The core of Earth is extremely hot. This heat sometimes breaks through the surface of the planet through volcanoes and geysers. In this experiment, create a volcano to learn about geothermal energy.

❯ **Build a volcano using clay or playdough around one of the bottles.** This will be your model volcano.

❯ **Put 3 teaspoons of baking soda in the bottle.**

❯ **Use a funnel to fill another plastic bottle about one-third full of vinegar.**

❯ **Add a few drops of red food coloring to the bottle with vinegar.** Then, add a good squeeze of dish soap.

❯ **Put on your eye protection!** Move your volcano and the bottles to the sink or bathtub or outside, where you can make a mess.

❯ **Tip the vinegar mixture onto the baking soda in your volcano bottle.** What happens? What does it look like? Record your observations in your science journal.

## TOOL KIT

- clay or playdough
- 2 plastic bottles (20 ounces)
- measuring spoons
- baking soda
- funnel
- vinegar
- red food coloring
- dish soap
- eye protection
- science journal

## Try This!

Use pop rocks and soda to make a noisy volcano. Fill your volcano container with soda. You can fill the container most of the way full (or experiment and start with three-quarters). Add a handful of pop rocks to the volcano and see what happens.

## THINK ABOUT IT!

When the baking soda is combined with the vinegar, there is a chemical reaction. This reaction produces a gas called carbon dioxide. The carbon dioxide gas creates pressure to throw out gas bubbles that exit the volcano like a real one.

# VISIT
# ROMAN BATHS

In a town called Bath, England, ancient Romans used geothermal energy to warm groundwater for the public bathing pools. This water could get as hot as 104 degrees Fahrenheit (96 degrees Celsius)! People built a large bathing complex around the hot springs and pools, and visitors believed the waters had healing powers. Sound like a good place to visit? Create a marketing tool so people will know about this kind of vacation!

❯ Do some research at the library and on the internet to learn more about the history of the Roman baths and the science of how the baths were heated.

❯ With paper and art supplies, design a website for the Roman baths for ancient visitors! What benefits might be important to people? Include pictures of what visitors might expect.

❯ Be sure to highlight the ways the Roman bath uses geothermal energy to heat the water. Visitors will want to know about this technology!

❯ Don't forget to write a list of frequently asked questions!

The Roman baths are now a tourist attraction, where **about 1.3 million people visit every year. But—no bathing allowed!** The site is more like a museum than a bath.

## Try This!

Share your website designs with your classmates and do a peer review of each other's work. What do you need to change and add to your website to make it more useful and attractive?

*TEXT TO* **WORLD**

Have you ever been to a hot spring or geyser? What was it like?

# Chapter 5

# VEGGIE
# POWER

**What do wind, solar, and water power all share? They all rely on energy from the sun. One more renewable energy source is also powered by the sun—bioenergy, which is generated from biomass.**

So far, most of what we have learned about renewable sources focused on how we make electricity. Remember, we use a lot of electricity! What else do we fuel that requires a lot of energy? Transportation.

**ESSENTIAL QUESTION**

What makes biomass a good alternative to fossil fuels?

We move goods and people around the world. From cars and airplanes to ships and trains, almost all these vehicles use fossil fuels. Since the early 1700s, fossil fuels have powered the way we move. All that burning of fossil fuels produces a lot of greenhouse gases, including carbon dioxide.

Where does the carbon dioxide go? It is released into the atmosphere. We need some carbon dioxide in the atmosphere for life to exist, but we've released so much of it that now there's an imbalance. This greenhouse gas has become a major driver of climate change here on planet Earth.

We could use other types of fuels to transport goods and people. Biomass is a renewable energy source made from **organic** matter such as leafy plants and **algae**. These **organisms** can be crushed, pressed, and squeezed, then mixed with other ingredients into renewable liquid biofuel, such as ethanol and biodiesel. These fuels can power our cars, ships, and airplanes, helping us to travel the world. Let's explore how organic matter can replace fossil fuels in powering our transportation sector.

## WORDS TO KNOW

**organic:** something that is or was living, such as wood, paper, grass, insects, and animals.

**algae:** a plant-like organism that turns light from the sun into energy but does not have leaves or roots.

**organism:** any living thing, such as a plant or animal.

**enzyme:** a substance produced by an organism that brings about a chemical reaction.

**herbaceous:** having the characteristics of a plant with a non-woody stem.

## FUELING LIFE

Bioenergy is energy from living things such as plants and animals. Bioenergy can come in different forms, including solid, liquid, and gas. We convert woody plants into solid biomass. We press and squeeze **herbaceous** plants and algae into liquid biofuels, such as ethanol and biodiesel.

## Measure It

Scientist Frances Arnold (1956– ) discovered a way to create **enzymes** for applications in alternative fuels, chemicals, and pharmaceuticals. Her work has led to the production of enzymes that function in airless environments, enabling the production of biofuels without expensive air-circulating equipment. She cofounded the biofuel company Gevo in 2005 and a second company, Provivi, in 2013 to develop green processes for agricultural and specialty chemicals.

# RENEWABLE ENERGY

## WORDS TO KNOW

**cell:** the basic part of a living thing. Cells are so small they can be seen only with a microscope. There are billions of cells in most living things.

**glucose:** a natural sugar occurring in plants that gives energy to living things.

**kilocalories:** the unit of measurement for energy in food.

We can even take food grease, animal waste, and garbage and convert them into usable forms of energy called biogas.

All these varieties of biofuels come from the energy stored in the organic matter in plants. All animals, including humans, use bioenergy. What happens if you skip breakfast the morning of a soccer game? Most people feel slow and sluggish if they go without a meal. The energy in food powers our bodies' daily activities.

**Bioenergy can replace the fossil fuels in plastic products, help us cook, and heat our homes.**

How do we get energy out of our food? Every **cell** in the human body—whether it's a muscle cell, brain cell, or heart cell—needs energy to work. This energy comes from the food we eat. We digest the food we eat by mixing it with our stomach fluids. This process breaks down the food into smaller and smaller pieces.

When the stomach digests food, the food breaks down into a simple sugar called **glucose**. Glucose is the energy that powers our cells. The intestines absorb glucose and then release it into our bloodstream. Once in the bloodstream, glucose can be used immediately.

An ethanol plant

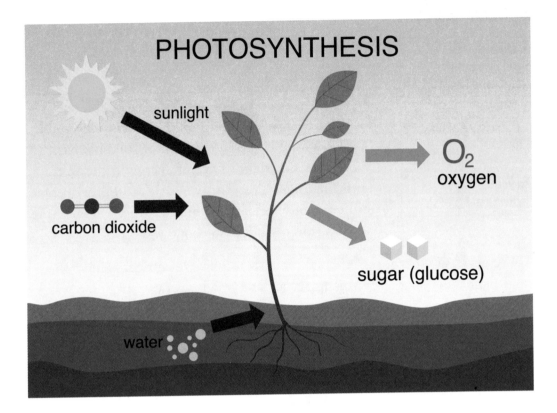

# PHOTOSYNTHESIS

sunlight

carbon dioxide

$O_2$
oxygen

sugar (glucose)

water

Plants use photosynthesis to produce glucose they can use for energy. During photosynthesis, plants use light energy from the sun to turn carbon dioxide and water into glucose. The waste product from this process is oxygen, which is what we breathe.

Bioenergy engineers are experts in biology, chemistry, and engineering. They figure out how to convert the sugars found in plants into usable energy—biofuel! We can use this biofuel to power cars, trucks, trains, and planes.

## Calorie Up!

We measure food energy in **kilocalories**, which we usually just call calories. Doctors recommend that the average child between the age of 4 and 8 eat 1,200 to 1,800 calories per day. The average child between 9 and 12 needs 1,600 to 2,200 calories per day. Doctors recommend adults eat around 2,000 calories a day, but the number of calories you need also depends on your weight and activity level.

## WORDS TO KNOW

**biologist:** a scientist who studies life and living things.

**corn stover:** plants left in a field after harvest.

**chemistry:** the science of how substances interact, combine, and change.

**biochemistry:** the study of chemistry in living things.

## TYPES OF BIOENERGY

A plant's biomass can be converted into different forms of energy, including solid biomass and liquid biofuel. Wood is the oldest form of solid biomass. Wood was the main source of energy in the world until the mid-1800s. Today, nearly 2.6 billion people still use wood for cooking and heating. Do you have a wood stove or know someone who does?

We also use other forms of solid biomass to power electrical plants. This solid biomass is made from materials such as wood, sawdust, and crop waste. These are often processed into briquettes, pellets, and charcoal.

**Biologists** and engineers are working to find new ways to convert the energy in organisms into liquid biofuels. **Corn stover** and plants— such as switchgrass, sugar cane, sugar beets, and algae—can be pressed and transformed into liquid biofuel using **chemistry** and **biochemistry** and their processes.

Much more energy is used to **refrigerate and prepare food in** the home than is used to grow food!

## Schools Lead the Way

Montana began using biomass boilers to heat its schools back in 2003. Today, more than 35 schools across the state are using biomass for heating. Montana is a forest-rich state, and using local timber helps to keep the communities and forests safe from wildfires. Well-managed forests that are harvested and replenished in sustainable ways can provide a long-term source of wood while keeping the atmosphere healthier through carbon storage. Students also get the opportunity to learn about this local, renewable energy source.

In 2021, biofuels provided about 5 percent of the energy in the United States. To use it, biofuel must be mixed with gas, but that still means a smaller percentage of fossil fuels are used when biofuel is in the mix.

## ETHANOL

Have you ever seen an "E85" symbol at a gas station? This is the symbol of a fuel blend of 85-percent ethanol. In the United States, almost all cars are running on a little bit of corn energy. That is because almost all gas stations in this country use a gasoline mixture that contains 10-percent ethanol. These cars are considered E10.

Flexible-fuel vehicles can use 85-percent ethanol, or E85. To determine if your vehicle runs on E85, check the gas cap or manual in your car. If your car runs on E85, the gas cap will be yellow, like the sun. Some cars also have labels. Next time your family goes to the gas station, see if you can find a flex-fuel pump that has E85.

Ethanol is the most widely used biofuel in the world. We can make ethanol from almost any plant. Some plants, however, are better than others. In Brazil, they use sugar cane to make ethanol. In France, they use sugar beets and wheat.

## WORDS TO KNOW

**manure:** animal waste.

**urea:** a waste product made by animal cells.

**decay:** to break down or rot.

**bacteria:** tiny organisms found in animals, plants, soil, and water that help decay food. Some bacteria are harmful, and others are helpful.

In the United States, we use mostly corn. Each plant produces a different amount of ethanol per acre of farmland used.

Biodiesel is another type of renewable liquid fuel. Biodiesel is mixed with diesel—a fossil fuel—to power diesel engines. Diesel engines are usually used in big machines or vehicles that require a lot of power. Many different plants can be used to create biodiesel.

**Crops that produce more gallons of biofuel per acre are more efficient.**

In the United States and Brazil, soybeans are the source of biodiesel. Head over to Europe, and the biodiesel comes from rapeseed. Biodiesel from jatropha, a common weed, is an increasingly popular source of energy in Haiti.

Jatropha

## WHAT SMELLS?

We even can make biofuels from animal waste and our own garbage. Large pig and cow farms produce a lot of animal waste, such as **manure** and **urea**. By capturing animal waste and turning it into biofuels, farmers can reduce the greenhouse gases emitted from the animal waste into the atmosphere. This reduces water and air pollution. Plus, if farmers can create their own fuel from animal manure, they don't need to purchase and use more fossil fuels. Farmers are using biodigesters. These are systems that take in farm waste and break it down into biogas and fertilizer.

Some organic materials **decay** with the help of **bacteria**. When organic matter decays, it produces methane. Landfills across the country emit methane into the atmosphere. And methane is a greenhouse gas!

At many landfills, engineers are creating ways to capture and utilize that methane gas. We can use methane from landfills to heat our homes and power our lights. In India, scientists are converting cow manure into methane gas to produce electricity.

# RENEWABLE ENERGY

## WORDS TO KNOW

**biorefinery:** a facility that produces transportation biofuels, power, and chemicals from biomass in an environmentally friendly way.

**fermentation:** a chemical reaction that breaks down food and other organic matter.

Another type of garbage that can be turned into biofuel is fast-food grease. Animal fats, greases, and vegetable oils can chemically react with alcohol to create biodiesel. The United States alone has around 50,000 fast-food restaurants, and worldwide there are more than 500,000! Imagine if we could use their waste to create diesel for our cars.

Everything we throw away took energy to make. Many types of waste, from garbage to manure to palm tree leaves and grass clippings, can be used to generate renewable energy. We can create biofuels from these different types of plants in many ways. The process takes place in **biorefineries**.

One process for converting plants to fuel is called **fermentation**. Have you ever opened your refrigerator and smelled something really bad?

Today two-thirds of all energy used to power U.S. naval bases comes **from renewable sources. This represents 1.2 GWs of energy—more than** enough to power the city of Orlando, Florida.

That is a sign that fermentation has occurred. It is usually the process of something going sour. In biorefineries, we want things to go sour—that means the organisms are breaking down into something we can use. Technicians cause this by mixing yeast with the starch from plants.

Waste-to-energy power plants are helping us utilize our waste and become more efficient. They take advantage of the things we normally consider waste and turn them into things we can use. This helps us to make a smaller impact on the planet.

**Plastic pollution is a major problem.** Not only is it ugly, it causes problems for wildlife. Read more in this article. What can you do to cut down on plastic pollution?

🔍 Nat Geo plastic pollution

## PLASTIC PLANTS

Did you know that many of your common household items are also made from fossil fuels? For example, plastics are made from fossil fuels.

Plastic water bottles are one example. The world throws away 500 billion water bottles every year. Many plastic bottles are not recycled and end up in landfills. What if plastics could be made from biomass?

What other things do you use that are made from plastic? Could we make these things without using fossil fuels? New bioproducts are being invented every day. Using crops, wastes, grasses, and forest residues, we can create new green chemicals, paper, and additives to help us make bioproducts. Two thousand pounds of recycled paper save up to 17 trees and use 50 percent less water than making new paper.

### Algae

Scientists are investigating ways to turn algae into biofuel. Algae are aquatic organisms living in ponds, lakes, oceans, and even wastewater. Algae use carbon dioxide to grow, which helps remove that greenhouse gas from the atmosphere. Algae also might provide a new type of biofuel. Estimates indicate that algae can produce 60 times more biofuel per acre than land-based plants.

## Fuel for Schools

The Fuel for Schools program began in Vermont during the 1980s. This program helps schools use biomass to save on energy bills. The program expanded in 2001 through the U.S. Department of Agriculture Forest Service. Today, schools from Idaho to Vermont are saving money by using biomass!

Look around your kitchen. What could be biobased? What do you see that's made of plastic that could easily be made of cloth, paper, wood, or some other bioproduct?

Biofuels can be solid, liquid, or gas and they can come from living plants, dead plants, or even your own garbage. The future for biofuels in the United States and the world is very bright.

## BIOENERGY TRADEOFFS

Bioenergy is probably the renewable energy source with the most tradeoffs. Liquid or dried biofuel requires a lot of processing. In addition, when we burn biomass, some carbon dioxide and other pollutants are released into the air. That makes bioenergy the only renewable energy source that releases significant quantities of carbon dioxide, a known greenhouse gas. Despite this, bioenergy is still preferable to fossil fuel use.

## More Green Careers!

### Biofuels Processing Technicians

Biofuels processing technicians are the experts you need to help with fermentation. These experimenters figure out how to create and mix biofuels in different ways and then monitor the results. A key part of their job is to keep records and stay safe. These are the people who help make E10 and E85 fuel. What will they create next?

### Bioprocess Engineers

Bioprocess engineers are leaders in creating new chemicals and products. They use math, chemistry, and biology to design and develop products such as bricks from biological material.

Growing and harvesting biomass requires the use of fuel. Tractors, trucks, fertilizer, and farmland are used, which contribute to the release of more carbon dioxide. Crops grown for biofuels can also consume large quantities of water.

These tradeoffs are considerable, but we are discovering new ways to turn our agricultural waste into fuel. The United States is a leader in growing corn. More than 90 million acres of land are used to grow corn. What do farmers do with the corn husks? These husks can be turned into biofuel.

Wood is an abundant bioenergy source found in our forests. Deforestation happens when too much forest is cut without replenishment, leaving a wasteland behind that isn't beneficial to anybody. Using wood means managing forests in ways that keep the land—and the atmosphere—healthy.

**ESSENTIAL QUESTION**

What makes biomass a good alternative to fossil fuels?

In the final chapter, we'll learn about the communities that are making wise energy choices and leading the way in the clean energy revolution.

# MAKE YOUR OWN
# LANDFILL

Landfills are where waste and garbage are buried between layers of soil. They are a crucial part of keeping our planet healthy. But there is a right way and a wrong way to construct one! Landfills need to be built so they can be safely contained far into the future.

> **Cut off the top of the plastic bottle.** This will be the container for your landfill.

> **Add a layer of soil to the bottom of the bottle.** This represents the natural soil of the land.

> **Add a layer of compacted clay or playdough on top of the soil.** It will act as a barrier that protects the ground water.

> **Cover the clay with a layer of plastic wrap or clear plastic.** You want to prevent liquid, or leachate, from draining from the landfill.

> **Spread out thin cotton balls over the plastic.** This will represent the special layer that separates solids and liquids in the runoff from the landfill.

> **Add a layer of gravel on top of the cotton balls.** The gravel and cotton collect the leachate as it exits the landfill.

> **Add a layer of trash to your landfill.** This can be from the recycling, a trash can, or a compost bin.

> **Cover the trash layer with soil.** This represents the daily covering of trash in a working landfill.

> **Add another layer of trash and soil and repeat this layering if there is room in the bottle.** When the bottle is two-thirds full, add another layer of clay or playdough on top of the last trash/soil layer.

## TOOL KIT

- empty plastic bottle
- scissors
- potting soil
- clay or playdough
- plastic wrap or clear plastic
- cotton balls
- gravel or aquarium gravel
- trash from recycling, trash can, or compost bin
- small plants or grass seeds (optional)
- science journal

## TEXT TO **WORLD**

Does your family compost? What do you do with the dirt from your compost pile?

> **Cover the clay with plastic wrap or clear plastic.** Add a layer of gravel on top of the plastic to act as drainage.

> **Top off the landfill with soil.** If you like, add plants or grass seeds to represent the top layer of a closed landfill.

> **It's time to observe!** Check your landfill every day for a week. What do you notice? Are there any changes?

> **Continue to check your landfill for another month.** Record your observations in your science journal.

## THINK ABOUT IT!

Why are landfills important? How do they serve the planet? Why is it important to keep waste out of landfills? How does reducing, reusing, and recycling help?

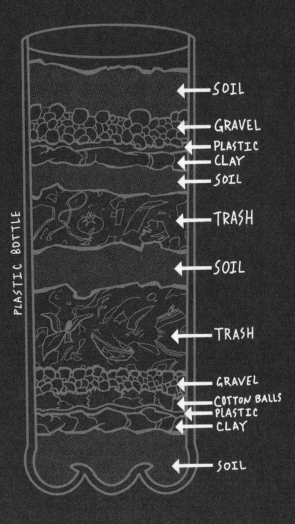

PLASTIC BOTTLE

SOIL
GRAVEL
PLASTIC
CLAY
SOIL
TRASH
SOIL
TRASH
GRAVEL
COTTON BALLS
PLASTIC
CLAY
SOIL

## Pack It Up

Much of what goes into landfills is packaging. Every time you have something shipped to your home, it has to be wrapped in a box or envelope, which gets thrown away and often ends up in a landfill. What's the alternative? Recycle whatever you can!

# FERMENTATION

**TOOL KIT**

- glass bottle
- plant matter or food waste
- eye protection
- science journal

Fermentation is the process by which organisms convert sugars into acids, gases, and alcohol. The common method for converting biomass into ethanol uses fermentation. Ethanol is the most widely used biofuel. It is mixed with petroleum to fuel cars and trucks around the world.

**Caution: Wear eye protection and keep your face away from the bottle mouth when opening!**

❯ **Fill a glass bottle with moist plant matter from your garden, yard, or a park.** Seal the bottle.

❯ **Place the bottle close to a gentle source of heat.** The sun or a heater will work well.

❯ **Check your bottle every day for a week.** What do you see? Record your observations in your science journal.

**Biomass has energy from the sun. Plants get energy from the sun through a process called photosynthesis. Animals get their energy indirectly from the sun by eating plants.**

❯ **After one week, open the bottle.** What do you hear? What do you smell? What do you see?

❯ **Note:** If you hear a slight hissing sound and a foul smell is released, the organic matter in the bottle has fermented and pressurized biogas has formed.

## THINK ABOUT IT!

How does this process of fermentation differ from composting? What gases are present or absent in fermentation?

**Biofuel has the power to change the world . . . literally!** Take a look at the process for making biofuel in this video. How do you think the biofuel industry will change the transportation industry?

🔎 Nat Geo biofuel

# YEAST BALLOON

Cellular respiration is the process through which cells convert sugars into energy. In this experiment, we will see how this conversion creates a gas, carbon dioxide. Yeast is a cheap source of energy that can convert sugar into carbon dioxide gas and alcohol.

> **Place 2 ounces of warm water into the bottle.**

> **Open the packet of yeast.** Using the funnel, carefully pour it into the bottle with the warm water.

> **Swirl the yeast and water together so they are mixed.** Are they easy to mix?

> **Add a teaspoon of sugar.** What happens?

> **Place the balloon over the top of the bottle.** Make sure that the balloon is tightly sealed around the opening of the bottle.

> **Swirl the mixture again.** Make sure it is well mixed.

> **Let the mixture in the bottle sit for about 20 minutes.** What happens to the balloon? Does it inflate?

## Try This!

Compare another type of sweetener besides table sugar to see how the amount of carbon dioxide production by the yeast is impacted. Try corn syrup, honey, or molasses.

## Yummy Fermentation

You know what else gets fermented? Yogurt! Tofu! Cottage cheese! People eat many different kinds of fermented foods. One reason is because of the taste, and another reason is health. Fermented foods are known to boost immunity and improve digestion.

# POWERING
# OUR FUTURE

IT'S IMPORTANT THAT WE KEEP DEVELOPING RENEWABLE ENERGY TECHNOLOGY!

IT SEEMS LIKE SUCH A SLOW CHANGE. IS IT WORTH IT?

IT DEFINITELY CAN BE SLOW, BUT EVERY SMALL STEP IS A STEP IN THE RIGHT DIRECTION.

**Our energy choices are not only an environmental issue. Our energy use impacts our public health, national security, and the economic systems of every country. Our energy choices as individuals and countries are impacting our future.**

It may seem like a big thing to tackle our energy choices, but we have already accomplished much in our history—from our initial use of geothermal energy to the invention of battery-powered cars. Reimagining and creating new ways to consume energy are important to reducing our greenhouse emissions. Each person is a part of the global community, and our individual choices have an impact on the rest of the world, not just ourselves.

### ESSENTIAL QUESTION

What's the best approach to ensure as many people as possible are using renewable energy?

By understanding our energy use, we can take actions that will reduce our carbon dioxide emissions and help solve the climate crisis.

Electricity was first sold in the United States in 1879 by the California Electric Light Company in San Francisco. A sewing machine, a fan, a kettle, and a toaster were some of the first home items to use electricity.

Today, electricity lights our homes, powers our computers for work, and enables us to watch our favorite television shows. What will we use to power our lives in the future?

Renewable energy sources can be used together to keep our planet healthy!

**Learn more about the energy revolution in this video.** Why is so much of our lives dependent on energy?

🔎 Introduction to Energy Literacy

## Global Connections

Sometimes, world events affect what we can do in our transition to renewables. The global pandemic that started in 2019 affected supply chains in a way that made it difficult for companies to get the parts they needed, such as computer chips, to build renewable energy systems. The Russian invasion of Ukraine that began in 2022 further disrupted supply chains. Plus, Russia cut off some of its gas exports, which caused havoc in many countries, especially those in Europe that relied on Russian gas for heat. As a result, some countries continue to use fossil fuels because it hasn't yet been possible to make a large-scale transition to new technologies.

# RENEWABLE ENERGY

**WORDS TO KNOW**

**power profile:** the different ways a city supplies energy to its population.

## MIXING IT UP

The mixture of energy supplied to a city or town is called its **power profile**. Think about your city or town. Does your energy come from renewables, fossil fuels, nuclear energy, or a mix? Which renewable energy do you think is the best choice for fueling cars, heating homes, producing electricity, warming water, and powering factories? What tradeoffs are involved?

Our world will need a mix of renewable energy technologies to work together to replace fossil fuels. But to succeed, these technologies will also need—us! The future of our planet and our communities is defined by our energy choices of today.

The U.S. Department of Energy had 17 national laboratories when this book was published in 2024. These laboratories make up the largest scientific research system in the world.

Renewable energy will help us create a healthier future and provide electricity to more people.

Every day, engineers work to improve the absorption of solar cells and redesign wind turbine blades. They research how to capture the power of waves and figure out efficient ways to use geothermal energy and to convert methane in landfills to electricity.

## Fuel Cell Electric Vehicles

Fuel cell electric vehicles (FCEVs) are powered by hydrogen. They are more efficient than conventional internal combustion engine vehicles and produce no harmful tailpipe emissions—they only emit water vapor and warm air. FCEVs and the hydrogen infrastructure to fuel them are in the early stages of implementation. The U.S. Department of Energy leads research efforts to make hydrogen-powered vehicles an affordable, environmentally friendly transportation option. Hydrogen is considered an alternative fuel under the Energy Policy Act of 1992 and qualifies for alternative fuel vehicle tax credits, which can bring down the cost of owning an FCEV for families.

# LIGHTS ON!

What does it mean to be more efficient? What do you do to make yourself more efficient in your schoolwork, homework, and sports?

Energy efficiency means trying to capture as much energy as possible and waste the least amount of it as possible. Anytime we capture or use energy, there is some waste. Being efficient means that we use processes or materials that reduce the amount of wasted energy.

**Daylight Savings time reduces energy consumption by about .34 percent.**

A solar panel is an excellent example of how efficiency can improve. During the 1970s, a solar panel could capture between 4 and 6 percent of the energy that struck its surface. That means 94 to 96 percent of the energy was lost as heat. In 2015, a high-efficiency research solar panel could capture as much as 40 percent of the energy that struck its surface.

# RENEWABLE ENERGY

## WORDS TO KNOW

**incandescent:** a source of electric light that works by heating a filament.

**light-emitting diodes (LEDs):** very efficient light bulbs that use less energy and last longer than incandescent bulbs.

**carbon footprint:** the total amount of carbon dioxide and other greenhouse gases emitted over the full life cycle of a product or service or by a person or family in a year.

The efficiency of solar panels has increased quite dramatically through research and new designs. In addition, the amount of material used in a 1-meter solar panel has decreased. Engineers are now more efficient when they build solar panels as well.

What about the lights in your house? Have you ever held your hand up close to a light bulb without touching it? What did you feel? An **incandescent** light bulb wastes 90 percent of the energy it uses. While generating light, it generates lots of heat! This heat is wasted. How many light bulbs do you have in your house? Turning off one 60-watt light bulb that normally is on eight hours a day saves 1,000 pounds of carbon dioxide during the lifetime of that bulb. Plus, your family will save money!

Incandescent bulbs are not efficient. Are there alternatives? Light bulbs are changing in terms of their efficiency and in the design of the bulbs. Now we have a choice about the type of light bulb we use. We can install **light-emitting diodes (LEDs)**.

LEDs are 90-percent efficient, so they lose only 10 percent of the energy they use! Not only do LEDs use less energy, they also last about 25 times longer than incandescent bulbs and provide more light.

## Calculate Your Carbon Footprint

The size of your **carbon footprint** indicates how much impact you have on the environment. Families can help reduce their carbon footprint by focusing on four major areas: housing and household energy use, transportation, personal habits, and recycling.

**You can calculate your own carbon footprint. Where can your family save energy?**

🔎 How Big Is Your Carbon Footprint?

In April 2022, the U.S. government issued a rule requiring all light bulbs sold to have a minimum standard of producing at least 45 lumens.

Regulation such as this makes it beneficial for companies to continue to push efficiency standards, which makes choosing efficiency more affordable for individuals and businesses.

Many outdoor lighting systems are using the power of solar. Small solar panels installed on lights for driveways, walkways, and gardens can help people navigate yards and neighborhoods at night. These solar lights are readily available and inexpensive. Homes are also using "smart" controls to turn off lights when not in use.

## Storing Energy

All of this renewable energy needs to be stored. How can we store solar or wind power for use after the sun goes down or the wind stops blowing? That is exactly the problem scientists are working to solve. Batteries that store energy on solar and wind farms could keep electricity flowing at all hours. Batteries come in all shapes and sizes. They are made of different materials. The type of material used to create the battery impacts the storage and flow of that energy. In designing batteries, engineers examine characteristics such as size, safety, cost, ability to be recycled, and heat generation.

## THE FUTURE OF DRIVING

What about transportation? How do we know if a gasoline-powered car is efficient? We measure efficiency in terms of miles per gallon. This measurement tells you how many miles you can typically drive on one gallon of gas. A car that can go 40 miles with one gallon is really efficient!

Making cars more efficient is an important job for automakers. We learned about vehicles that use biofuels, but there are other options, such as all-electric vehicles (EVs) or plug-in hybrids (PHEVs). Both use electricity to power the car, but hybrid plug-in cars use gasoline as a back-up fuel. As of 2022, 2 million electric cars and about 860,000 PHEVs are being driven in the United States.

In 1938, a discovery was made in Iraq of a 5-inch pottery jar **containing a copper cylinder encased in an iron rod. It's** thought to be an ancient battery.

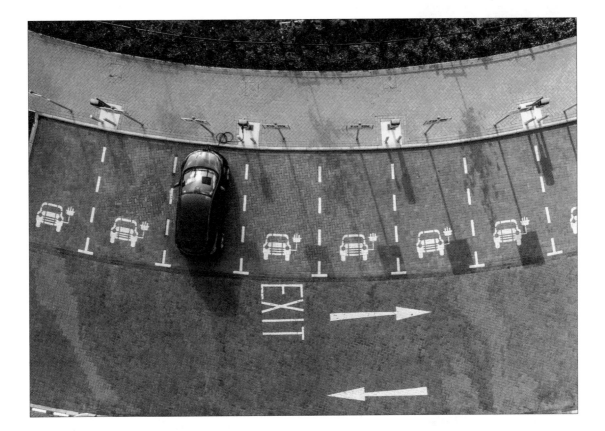

In many regions, electric charging stations are placed at regular intervals along a stretch of road, which allows electric cars to travel long distances. Just like fossil fuel cars, electric cars can stop at a "fuel station" and recharge. The goal is to get more EVs on the road, so increasing the number of charging stations is an important step. Creating the charging infrastructure for EVs takes a mix of federal, state, and local policies.

As the charging station infrastructure **becomes stronger, electric delivery** vehicles are becoming more commonplace.

Many states have individual electrification plans that can be reviewed to see how far your battery-powered car could go. We need to be strategic about charging locations—for example, placing them at grocery stores, schools, or libraries.

**WORDS TO KNOW**

**transparent:** clear or see-through. A description of matter that allows light rays to pass through it.

**translucent:** allowing some light to pass through, semi-transparent. A description of matter that scatters the light rays that pass through it.

**opaque:** something that you cannot see through; the opposite of transparent.

## LIVING GREEN

Engineers are also working to design buildings in ways that waste less energy. Can you think of ways that a building could be more energy efficient? Many states and communities offer free energy efficiency audits of homes.

An expert can come and point out places that need more insulation, windows that could be replaced with more efficient ones, and appliances that use more energy than they need to.

Replacing leaky windows with airtight ones is one way to make a building more efficient. For example, many homes and businesses are using smart glass technologies. These alter the amount of light transmitted, making them appear as **transparent**, **translucent**, or **opaque**. This technology helps balance the benefits of natural light with the need for energy conservation and privacy.

The international organization Clean Energy Education & Empowerment, sometimes known as C3E, is dedicated to helping women advance in clean energy fields. Scientists, engineers, environmental advocates, and policy leaders are part of the organization.

Insulation is another way to make a building more efficient. A long time ago, people used newspaper to insulate the walls of buildings—now we know there are better ways! How about adding green space to roofs? Gardens on the tops of buildings provide great places for families and communities to share. Trees and plants also help to absorb carbon dioxide from the air. In addition, green roofs improve the insulation of a building, making it more energy efficient.

Anything that can be done to make buildings more energy efficient saves money and reduces our carbon emissions. Buildings that follow some of the best practices for protecting the environment are designated as Leadership in Energy & Environmental Design (LEED) buildings. LEED encourages people to build energy-efficient buildings. Are there LEED buildings in your community? Do some research to find out and then go visit one.

All this research and these new designs help us be more efficient. But we need people, school officials, and businesspeople asking for and using renewable technologies. You, too, can join the clean-energy movement by taking energy-saving actions.

## ACTIONS TO SAVE ENERGY

How do your energy choices affect the future? Thinking about our actions is important for our clean future. It's not just researchers, engineers, and inventors helping to make renewable technology more efficient. All of us can take action in our homes, schools, and businesses to waste less energy.

# RENEWABLE ENERGY

Take a look at this list of actions you can do to help reduce climate change!

- **Unplug electronics,** including your computer, tablet, or cell phone.

- **Turn on the energy-efficient light bulbs** such as LEDs only when and where you really need them. Turn off the lights whenever you leave a room.

- **Have your school or classroom create a garden.** The garden can help you learn about energy and even grow food.

- **Plant trees.** Did you know that one of the easiest things we can do to help clean our air and combat climate change is plant trees? Plant trees in your school's playground and outside areas. One tree can absorb nearly 1 ton of carbon dioxide in its lifetime.

This library in the capitol city of Warsaw in Poland has a rooftop garden and solar panels.

- **Use power strips.** When you have a lot of devices to plug in, power strips conserve and use energy efficiently. With the flick of a switch, you can turn everything off at once.

- **Shut your curtains** on hot, sunny days to help keep your room cool.

- **On a sunny day, hang your clothes outside** to dry instead of using the dryer.

- **Walk or use a bike** instead of taking your car. Ride a bus or carpool.

- **Keep the refrigerator door closed.** It releases a lot of energy when open.

- **Reuse containers.** Don't throw out that plastic container from the restaurant! Reuse it tomorrow for lunch.

- **Do research** with a parent to identify how you can regulate your home temperature.

- **Think about what you eat.** It takes a lot of energy to produce a pound of meat. One serving of beef creates as many units of greenhouse gases as driving 49 miles! Eating less meat each year will make a difference.

- **Get involved!** Look for ways to advocate for renewable energy. That might involve marching, writing letters and emails, planting trees, creating a community garden, or taking part in citizen science projects.

- **Look for the Energy Efficiency Rating stickers on appliances.** The higher the number, the more efficient the product. These labels can help your family make good energy choices in your home.

Studies show that as many as one in four **workers will have jobs in the renewable** energy or energy-efficiency fields by 2030. Will you be one of them?

**WORDS TO KNOW**

**carbon neutral:** when the use of energy adds no carbon to the atmosphere.

## CLEAN ENERGY COMMUNITIES

In many places around the world, renewables are already powering communities. Local governments are leading the way. In 2020, Scotland produced more than 97 percent of its electricity from renewables. Iceland uses a combination of hydropower and geothermal power to provide almost 100 percent of Iceland's electricity needs. In fact, geothermal power heats 9 out of 10 Icelandic homes.

Morocco is now home to the world's biggest concentrated solar farm, located in the Sahara Desert. This farm is the size of 3,500 football fields and generates enough electricity to power a city twice the size of Marrakesh.

Small islands around the world are also making major shifts toward renewable energy use. One island in Denmark, called Samsø, gets 100 percent of its electricity from renewable energy. Samsø has nearly 4,000 people and all its electricity comes from biomass, solar, and wind. Other islands, such as Tilos in Greece and the island of Jeju of South Korea, are aiming to be **carbon neutral**. Islands are important leaders in this area. They often see the first impacts of climate change—such as flooding, extreme storms, and eroding coastlines—and have high energy costs because fossil fuels need to come to them from long distances.

### What is Carbon Neutral?

Carbon neutral means having a balance between the amount of carbon released and the amount of carbon absorbed in the atmosphere. For example, cars emit a lot of carbon dioxide into the air. Trees and the ocean are great absorbers of that carbon. We may need to plant more trees and drive less to help balance the amount of carbon we release.

In 2020, renewable energy sources generated 21 percent of all the electricity in the United States. This is a significant milestone! However, we can always do more. Businesses are leading the way in investing and using renewable energy. Intel, Apple, Walmart, Kohl's, and the National Hockey League are all using renewable energy. Companies such as Google, Microsoft, Dow Chemical, and Hewlett-Packard (HP) are also working to make their data centers run on renewable energy. The U.S. Postal Service intends to have more than 60,000 electric vehicles delivering mail by 2028.

**Nearly 900 million people in the world have no access to electricity. How do they produce heat and light? They use other sources, such as wood, candles, and oil lamps.**

Another way cities around the world are going green is by making public transportation electric or completely free to use, which helps to encourage communities to use it. Countries—from the smallest of islands, such as the Maldives, to the global economies of France and South Korea—continue to lead in the energy transition. More than 70 percent of countries continue to improve their energy access and security. Cities are being designed and built to be more walkable, with shops such as grocery stores near schools and houses. Making transportation free and cities more walkable reduces daily emissions.

Renewable energy is part of the answer to many of our climate change problems. By working together as a global community committed to reducing our dependence on fossil fuels, we can enjoy the benefits of power from solar, wind, water, geothermal, and biofuel sources while ensuring our planet will be healthy for centuries into the future!

**ESSENTIAL QUESTION**

What's the best approach to ensure as many people as possible are using renewable energy?

TEXT TO **WORLD**

What kinds of renewable energy would work best for your household?

# DESIGN A CITY
## POWERED BY RENEWABLE ENERGY

We are seeing more and more communities that are designed with the environment in mind. From green office buildings to rooftop gardens to net-zero homes, the future of where we live is energy efficient! What kind of green city might you design?

> **Think about what you need for a community to be as energy efficient as possible.** What kinds of buildings do you need? What types of homes? What will your community members do for transportation, food, and work? Write your plans in your science journal.

> **Using your plans, sketch buildings that can be powered by renewable energy.** Where should they be built?

> **Draw the vehicles in your community that will be powered by bioenergy or electricity.** Don't forget charging stations!

> **Add features to your city.** Make it more friendly to pedestrians.

> **Identify any spaces where food can be grown.** Use your imagination!

> **Label the renewable energy sources your community uses.** What benefits and drawbacks do you predict?

## Try This!

Let's get detailed. Think about how the environment impacts the design of a city. Do you need buildings that can withstand large amounts of snow or bridges to cross waterways? Are you in a sunny location so solar panels could power the city? Add in some details of the city's environment to show how the design of the city may change.

**absorb:** to soak up a liquid or take in energy, heat, light, or sound.

**acid rain:** rain that contains pollution from burning fuels.

**aeronautical engineer:** a person who designs and tests aircraft.

**agrivoltaics:** the use of land for both solar power generation and agricultural use.

**algae:** a plant-like organism that turns light from the sun into energy but does not have leaves or roots.

**anemometer:** a device that measures wind speed and pressure.

**aquatic:** related to water.

**archaeological:** having to do with archaeology, the study of ancient people through the objects they left behind.

**atmosphere:** the mixture of gases surrounding Earth.

**atmospheric pressure:** the amount of force pressing down on you by the weight of air.

**atom:** a small piece of matter with a nucleus in the center surrounded by electrons.

**bacteria:** tiny organisms found in animals, plants, soil, and water that help decay food. Some bacteria are harmful, and others are helpful.

**battery:** a device that stores and produces electricity using chemicals.

**BCE:** put after a date, BCE stands for Before Common Era and counts down to zero. CE stands for Common Era and counts up from zero. This book was printed in 2024 CE.

**biochemistry:** the study of chemistry in living things.

**bioenergy:** energy created from recently living matter, such as trees and other plants.

**biologist:** a scientist who studies life and living things.

**biomass:** plant materials and animal waste used as fuel.

**biorefinery:** a facility that produces transportation biofuels, power, and chemicals from biomass in an environmentally friendly way.

**carbon:** a kind of atom that is the building block of most living things, as well as diamonds, charcoal, and graphite.

**carbon dioxide (CO$_2$):** a gas formed by the burning of fossil fuels, the rotting of plants and animals, and the breathing out of animals, including humans.

**carbon footprint:** the total amount of carbon dioxide and other greenhouse gases emitted over the full life cycle of a product or service or by a person or family in a year.

**carbon neutral:** when the use of energy adds no carbon to the atmosphere.

**cell:** the basic part of a living thing. Cells are so small they can be seen only with a microscope. There are billions of cells in most living things.

**chemistry:** the science of how substances interact, combine, and change.

**civilization:** a community of people that is advanced in art, science, and government.

**climate change:** a change in the long-term weather patterns of a place.

**collaboration:** working together.

**compost:** to recycle food scraps and dead plants and put them back in the soil.

**concentrated solar power:** when a large amount of solar energy is concentrated using mirrors.

**condense:** when a gas cools down and changes into a liquid.

**continental crust:** Earth's crust on which land is found.

**convection current:** the movement of hot air or liquid rising and cold air or liquid sinking.

**core:** the innermost layer of Earth consisting of a solid inner core and a liquid outer core.

**corn stover:** plants left in a field after harvest.

**corrode:** to rust, or wear away metal by a chemical reaction.

**crops:** plants grown for food and other uses.

**crust:** the outer layer of Earth.

**current:** the steady flow of water in one direction or the flow of electricity.

**dam:** a barrier across a river to hold back and control the water.

**data:** facts and observations about something.

**decay:** to break down or rot.

**dense:** how tightly the matter in an object is packed.

**direct relationship:** a relationship where both variables increase or decrease together.

**drought:** a long period of unusually low rainfall that can harm plants and animals.

**earthquake:** a sudden movement in the outer layer of Earth, which releases stress built up from the motion of Earth's plates.

**ecosystem:** a community of living and nonliving things and their environment. Living things are plants, animals, and insects. Nonliving things are soil, rocks, and water.

**efficient:** wasting as little time as possible.

**electricity:** a form of energy caused by the movement of tiny particles that powers lights, appliances, and many other electric devices.

**electron:** a particle in an atom with a negative charge.

**emission:** something that is sent or given out, such as smoke, gas, heat, or light.

**emitter:** a device that sends or gives out something, such as smoke, gas, heat, or light.

**energy:** the ability or power to do work or cause change.

**energy transition:** a period during which the dominant resource used to produce energy is replaced by other resources.

**engineering:** the use of science and math in the design and construction of things.

**environment:** everything in nature, living and nonliving, including plants, animals, soil, rocks, and water.

**enzyme:** a substance produced by an organism that brings about a chemical reaction.

**equator:** an imaginary line around the earth, halfway between the North and South Poles.

**evaporation:** the process by which a liquid becomes a gas.

**expand:** to increase in size or to take up more space.

**fermentation:** a chemical reaction that breaks down food and other organic matter.

**fossil:** the remains of any living thing, including animals and plants, that have been preserved in rock.

**fossil fuels:** coal, oil, and natural gas. These energy sources come from the fossils of plants and animals that lived millions of years ago.

**generate:** to produce energy.

**generator:** a machine that converts mechanical energy into electricity.

**geothermal energy:** energy from below Earth's surface that can heat or cool using differences in temperature above and below ground.

**geothermal heat pump:** a device that gets energy from underground to heat or cool buildings.

**geyser:** a hot spring under pressure that shoots boiling water or steam into the air.

**glacier:** a sheet of ice that slowly moves downhill due to gravity.

**global warming:** a gradual increase in the average temperature of Earth's atmosphere and its oceans.

**glucose:** a natural sugar occurring in plants that gives energy to living things.

**goods:** things made or grown that can be bought, sold, or traded.

**gravitational effect:** the force of attraction between two masses.

**gravity:** a force that pulls objects to the earth.

**Great Plains:** a large area of flat grassland in the center of the United States between the Mississippi River and the Rocky Mountains. Another word for this grassland is prairie.

**greenhouse gases:** gases in the earth's atmosphere that trap heat.

**herbaceous:** having the characteristics of a plant with a non-woody stem.

**horizontal axis of rotation:** the movement of wind horizontally across the blades of a turbine.

**hot spring:** a natural pool of water heated by hot or molten rock. Hot springs are found in areas with active volcanoes.

**humid:** a weather condition marked by large amounts of water vapor in the atmosphere.

**hydroelectric power plant:** a power plant that uses moving water to power a turbine generator to produce electricity.

**hydrokinetic:** related to the motion of fluids.

**hydropower:** energy produced by the movement of water.

**incandescent:** a source of electric light that works by heating a filament.

**Industrial Revolution:** a period during the eighteenth and nineteenth centuries when large cities and factories began to replace small towns and farming.

**infrared light:** an invisible type of light with a longer wavelength than visible light, which can also be felt as heat.

**inverse relationship:** a relationship where one variable increases as the other decreases.

**inverter:** a device that converts an electrical charge into a type of electricity that can be used in homes.

**irrigation:** a system for bringing water to farmland.

**jet stream:** a band of strong wind that blows from west to east across the globe.

**kilocalories:** the unit of measurement for energy in food.

**kinetic energy:** energy created from motion.

**light-emitting diodes (LEDs):** very efficient light bulbs that use less energy and last longer than incandescent bulbs.

**lumens:** the unit of measurement for brightness.

**mantle:** the layer of Earth between the crust and core.

**manure:** animal waste.

**marine:** found in the ocean or having to do with the ocean.

**matter:** anything that has weight and takes up space. Almost everything is made of matter!

**medieval:** a period of time between the fall of the Roman Empire and the Renaissance, roughly between the years 350 and 1450. Also known as the Middle Ages.

**mineral:** a solid, nonliving substance found in the earth and in water, such as gold, salt, or copper.

**nonrenewable energy:** a form of energy that can be used up, that we can't make more of, such as oil.

**nuclear energy:** energy produced by a nuclear reaction, typically the splitting of an atom.

**nuclear fission:** when the nucleus of an atom splits and releases energy in a nuclear reaction.

**nuclear fusion:** when the nuclei of two atoms combine and release energy in a nuclear reaction.

**nutrients:** substances in food, water, and soil that living things need to live and grow.

**oceanic crust:** Earth's crust that lies under the oceans.

**oceanographer:** a scientist who studies the ocean.

**offshore:** describes a wind farm that is built in the ocean, either on the ocean floor or floating on the water.

**onshore:** describes a wind farm that is built on land.

**opaque:** something that you cannot see through; the opposite of transparent.

**organic:** something that is or was living, such as wood, paper, grass, insects, and animals.

**organism:** any living thing, such as a plant or animal.

**passive solar power:** the use of black surfaces or pipes to capture the heat of solar energy.

**PhD:** stands for doctor of philosophy. A PhD is the highest degree in an area of study given by a college or university.

**photon:** a particle of energy in sunlight.

**photosynthesis:** the process plants use to convert the sun's energy into food.

**photovoltaics:** technology used to convert sunlight into electricity.

**physics:** the science of how matter and energy work together.

**pollinator:** an insect or other animal that transfers pollen from the male part of a flower to the female part of a flower. Pollen is a fine, yellow powder produced by flowering plants that is needed by a flower to make a seed.

**pollution:** harmful materials that damage the air, water, and soil.

**power profile:** the different ways a city supplies energy to its population.

**precipitation:** condensed water vapor that falls to the earth's surface in the form of rain, snow, sleet, or hail.

**pump storage:** a system for moving water using extra electricity, storing the water, and then allowing the water to flow through turbines to create electricity when it's needed.

**recycle:** to shred, squash, pulp, or melt items so they can be used to create new products.

**reflect:** to bounce off and redirect something that hits a surface, such as heat, light, or sound.

**renewable energy:** a form of energy that naturally replenishes itself, including the energy of the sun or the wind.

**reservoir:** a man-made or natural body of water that's stored for future use.

**resource:** things found in nature, such as wood or gold, that people can use.

**river delta:** a collection of rocks and soil at the mouth of a river.

**rotation:** a turn around a fixed point.

**satellite:** an object that circles another object in space. Also, a device that circles Earth and transmits information.

**seismic:** related to earthquakes.

**shaft:** a bar that connects gears and transfers power from one gear to another.

**silicon:** an element used in solar panels that can interact with photons to release electrons.

**slinky loop:** a system of overlapping plastic tubing that carries water heated by geothermal energy into buildings and out again.

**smart grid:** a computer-based remote control and automated system for delivering electricity that includes two-way interaction between the source of the electricity and those using it.

**smog:** fog combined with smoke or other pollutants.

**solar cell:** a device that converts the energy of the sun into electrical energy.

**solar eclipse:** when the moon moves between the sun and the earth, blocking the sun's light.

**solar energy:** energy from the sun.

**solar panel:** a device that converts energy from the sun to electricity.

**solar system:** the sun, the eight planets, and their moons, together with smaller bodies. The planets orbit the sun.

**solar thermal:** technology used to heat water with energy from the sun and convert it into electricity.

**solar tracker:** a device that allows mounted solar panels to follow the movement of the sun.

**spawning ground:** where an animal goes to lay its eggs.

**species:** a group of living things that are closely related and can produce young.

**STEAM:** an acronym that stands for science, technology, engineering, mathematics, and art.

**submersible:** a boat that can go below the surface of the water.

**super magnet:** the strongest type of permanent magnets ever made.

**sustainable:** a process or resource that can be used without being completely used up or destroyed.

**technology:** the tools, methods, and systems used to solve a problem or do work.

**tidal power:** another form of hydropower, using tides.

**tide:** the daily rising and falling of ocean water, based on the pull of the moon's and sun's gravity.

**topsoil:** the upper layer of soil.

**toxic:** poisonous, harmful, or deadly.

**trade winds:** winds that blow almost continually toward the equator from the northeast north of the equator and from the southeast south of the equator.

**translucent:** allowing some light to pass through, semi-transparent. A description of matter that scatters the light rays that pass through it.

**transparent:** clear or see-through. A description of matter that allows light rays to pass through it.

**turbine:** a machine with rotating blades that changes one type of energy to another, such as wind energy into electricity.

**ultraviolet (UV) light:** a type of light with a short wavelength that can't be seen with the naked eye.

**urea:** a waste product made by animal cells.

**vent:** a hole that lets air escape. In nature, a vent is a crack in the earth's surface that lets hot gas escape.

**vertical axis of rotation:** the movement of wind vertically across the blades of a turbine.

**visible light:** light that the human eye can see.

**water cycle:** the natural recycling of water through evaporation, condensation, precipitation, and collection.

**water vapor:** the gas form of water in the air.

**water wheel:** a wheel with paddles that spins when water flows over it. The energy can be used to power machines or lift water.

**watts:** the unit of measurement for electricity. A kilowatt-hour (kWh) is a unit of work or energy equal to the amount produced by one kilowatt (1,000 watts) in one hour.

**wavelength:** the spacing of sound or light waves.

**wind energy:** energy from the wind that can be transformed into electricity.

**windmill:** a device that converts the energy of the wind to mechanical energy.

## Metric Conversions

Use this chart to find the metric equivalents to the English measurements in this book. If you need to know a half measurement, divide by two. If you need to know twice the measurement, multiply by two. How do you find a quarter measurement? How do you find three times the measurement?

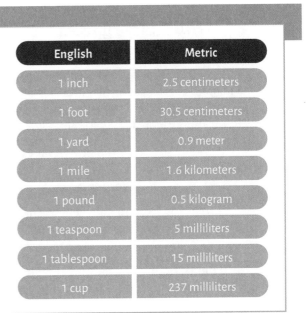

| English | Metric |
| --- | --- |
| 1 inch | 2.5 centimeters |
| 1 foot | 30.5 centimeters |
| 1 yard | 0.9 meter |
| 1 mile | 1.6 kilometers |
| 1 pound | 0.5 kilogram |
| 1 teaspoon | 5 milliliters |
| 1 tablespoon | 15 milliliters |
| 1 cup | 237 milliliters |

## BOOKS

Mooney, Carla. *Climate in Crisis: Changing Coastlines, Severe Storms, and Damaging Drought.* Nomad Press, 2022.

Mittermeier, Cristina. *Rebel Girls Climate Warriors: 25 Tales of Women Who Protect the Earth.* Rebel Girls, 2022.

Minoglio, Andrea. *Our World Out of Balance: Understanding Climate Change and What We Can Do.* Blue Dot Kids Press, 2021.

Sneideman, Joshua, and Erin Twamley. *Climate Change: The Science Behind Melting Glaciers and Warming Oceans with Hands-On Science Activities.* Nomad Press, 2020.

Clark, Stacy. *Planet Power: Explore the World's Renewable Energy.* Barefoot Books, 2021.

## WEBSITES

**Office of Energy Efficiency & Renewable Energy: energy.gov/education**
Find videos, lessons, and activities about energy.

**National Energy Education Development Project: need.org**
Explore lesson plans, projects, and education about energy.

**Green Education Foundation: greeneducationfoundation.org**
A nonprofit organization that provides curriculum and resources to K-12 students and teachers worldwide with the goal of challenging youth to think holistically and critically about global environmental, social, and economic concerns and solutions

**Alliance to Save Energy: ase.org**
A nonprofit organization that promotes energy efficiency worldwide through research, education and advocacy

**"What You Need to Know About Energy": needtoknow.nas.edu/energy**
This interactive website from the National Academies of Sciences, Engineering, and Medicine is a reliable source for information and science related to energy.

**The National Academies YouTube channel: youtube.com/user/nationalacademies**
A great resource for energy and climate change videos

**U.S. Energy Information Administration - Energy for Kids: https://www.eia.gov/kids**
Offers relevant games and good information

**U.S. Department of Energy - Energy Saver: energy.gov/energysaver/energy-saver**
Beyond providing information about low-cost ways to lower household energy bills, the site also offers information about local tax credits, rebates, and energy-efficiency financing that might be available in different communities.

## ESSENTIAL QUESTIONS

**Introduction:** Why is it important to find and use renewable energy sources in place of fossil fuels?

**Chapter 1:** How can we use the sun to produce energy here on Earth?

**Chapter 2:** Why can wind be considered another form of solar energy?

**Chapter 3:** How does water generate electricity?

**Chapter 4:** How can we use heat from inside Earth to power our lives on the surface of the planet?

**Chapter 5:** What makes biomass a good alternative to fossil fuels?

**Chapter 6:** What's the best approach to ensure as many people as possible are using renewable energy?

# QR CODE GLOSSARY

**Page 9**: youtube.com/watch?v=fHztd6k5ZXY

**Page 11**: cleanet.org/clean/literacy/energyquiz.html

**Page 12**: youtube.com/watch?v=Bdw8czqc4G4

**Page 17**: youtu.be/bPwvS5V5RW4

**Page 18**: darksky.org

**Page 26**: youtube.com/watch?v=F6h0jwxZcM8

**Page 35**: youtu.be/-s7zOubwXmc

**Page 35**: youtube.com/watch?v=EYYHfMCw-FI

**Page 37**: youtu.be/o203JXAnSA0

**Page 42**: earth.nullschool.net

**Page 46**: eerscmap.usgs.gov/uswtdb

**Page 54**: youtube.com/watch?v=tpigNNTQix8

**Page 61**: smap.jpl.nasa.gov

**Page 65**: nid.sec.usace.army.mil

**Page 71**: youtube.com/watch?v=Q8oZoVC8rGc

**Page 73**: volcanodiscovery.com/volcano-map.html

**Page 73**: experience.arcgis.com/experience/b4e8785f0f75464b9e08547ccf0b18d7

**Page 74**: youtube.com/watch?v=HCDVN7DCzYE

**Page 77**: youtube.com/watch?v=mCRDf7QxjDk&list=PLACD8E92715335CB2&index=6

**Page 78**: energy.gov/articles/mapping-geothermal-heat-flow-and-existing-plants

**Page 91**: kids.nationalgeographic.com/science/article/plastic-pollution

**Page 96**: education.nationalgeographic.org/resource/edu-bio-fuels

**Page 99**: youtube.com/watch?v=Zq3EFJ05fec

**Page 102**: energystar.gov/ia/products/globalwarming/downloads/amazing/Team_ENERGY_STAR_Games_Final.pdf?b78f-b568w